Uncommon Knowledge

An Introduction to
Past Life & Health Readings

Uncommon Knowledge

An Introduction to
Past Life & Health Readings

Edited by

Barbara Condron, D.M., B.J.

Essays by
Daniel R. Condron, D.M., M.S.
Laurel Jan Clark, D.M., B.A.
Sheila Benjamin, D.M., B.S.
Pam Blosser, D.M., B.A.
Paul Blosser, B.A.

SOM Publishing
Windyville, Missouri 65783

Other SOM titles about the readings

- **The Work of the Soul**
- **Going in Circles: Our Search for a Satisfying Relationship**
- **What Will I Do Tomorrow: Probing Depression**
- **Permanent Healing**

soon to be released...

- **First Opinion**

Revised Edition, October 1996

ISBN: 0-944386-19-9

Library of Congress Catalogue Number Pending

Cover Design by Sharka Glet

If you desire to learn more about the research and
teachings in this book, write to School of Metaphysics,
National Headquarters, Windyville, Missouri 65783.
Or call 417-345-8411.
Visit us on the Internet at http://www.som.org

Knowledge

...is the food of the soul.
— Socrates (399 B.C.)

...is the true organ of sight, not the eyes.
— Panchatantra (5 A.D.)

...is the wing whereby we fly to Heaven.
— William Shakespeare (1591)

...in truth, is the great sun in the firmament.
Life and power are scattered with all its beams.
— Daniel Webster (1830)

...is happiness, because to have knowledge -
broad deep knowledge - is to know true ends
from false, and lofty things from low.
To know the thoughts and deeds
that have marked man's progress
is to feel the great heart-throbs of humanity
through the centuries; and if one does not feel
in these pulsations a heavenward striving,
one must indeed be deaf to the harmonies of life.
— Helen Keller (1940)

...begets knowledge.
The more I see, the more impressed I am -
not with what we know - but with how tremendous
the areas are that are as yet unexplored.
— Lt. Col. John H. Glenn, Jr. (1980)

FOREWORD

In today's world, information concerning the affairs of mankind comes to us at a sometimes overwhelming pace. In our search for Self awareness, modern technology provides the means to have immediate access to what is happening thousands of miles across the globe. From a politically motivated assassination attempt to motion picture awards, from a medical advancement in conquering disease to Olympic sports events, if it holds import for humanity the events are publicized almost as quickly as they occur thus becoming common knowledge.

Daily media inform us of the latest discovery and statistics in areas that concern all of us. Yet it seems our ability to disseminate information is unequal to our ability to assimilate it. Thus what could be a source of greater contentment, peace, and security becomes a stimulus for greater confusion, fear, and misunderstanding. Too often we find that increased knowledge of the world around us does not lend itself readily to a growth in Self awareness which can produce the kind of world we want for ourselves and our children.

Consider, researchers estimate the average person in the United States will have three or four careers during his lifetime, and reports show most are not equipped to effectively handle these changes in life. It is becoming common knowledge that we tend to repeat patterns throughout our lives, for instance the spouse we choose tends to have more relevance to our same-sex parent than we probably originally intended. Scientists continue to find no reason for the aging of the physical body, yet aging does indeed occur. Amid all the research man pursues, and no matter how many physical actions and reactions he identifies, the profound question too often remaining unanswered is WHY?! Even with the plethora of information available, we still find this most important question in life unanswered.

Imagine, how would your life change if you knew the purpose for your existence? How would this knowledge affect your choices in life, your relationships with others, your general attitude toward living?

How would your consciousness change if you could remember your existence before the birth of your physical body in this lifetime? Would it alter your awareness of the meaning of physical life and open doors to new knowledge of the continuity of Self as spirit? Could it answer the many questions physical life leaves unanswered?

How would your attitude change if you knew the governing power of your manner of thinking – not only in professional or social realms but in the quality of your mental, emotional, and physical health? Would freedom from fear of illness encourage you to think, and therefore act, more productively and positively?

For a quarter of a century, researchers at the School of Metaphysics have dedicated their efforts to expanding mankind's knowledge of himself and his universe. They are committed to answering the "why's" of life and cultivating the "how-to's" for a more enlightened existence. What is being discovered is destined to change the way we see ourselves and our world.

Through years of concentration and meditation practices, individuals have honed the mind to achieve deeper and deeper states of consciousness. Lucid dreaming, psi development, intuitive skills, and accumulated wisdom are experienced within these levels of awareness. So is the universal memory of where all souls have been and knowledge of their destiny.

There are those who have sufficiently prepared themselves to be trained to access universal memory and report what is perceived. These past life accounts – known as *readings* – do much more than satisfy curiosity or boost the ego. They describe the karmic bonds that hold the soul earthbound hereby revealing what needs to occur for the soul to progress. This uncommon knowledge conveys the reason that soul has taken physical form and the work it intends for the present life.

There are also those who have sufficiently prepared and who have trained to perceive and describe the energies emanating from a person. These energies comprise the human aura. They are mental, emotional, and physical in composition and can be perceived in deep states of consciousness. *Reading* the health aura reveals more than the state of the body, it describes how consciousness is being used and misused thus determining the point of origin of dis-ease. Specific ways of thinking produce specific states of health. This uncommon knowledge empowers the individual to control his mind and body, to establish health and enhance the quality of life.

The considerable revelatory knowledge that has been imparted through the years is truly amazing. For instance, uncovering proof of previous life existences *indirectly* occurred as a result of SOM research into mankind's potential and the development of consciousness. It was not the intention to prove the reality of previous existences or the continuity of life or the existence of the soul, yet this is transpiring. The very nature of the information flowing from the inner levels during readings lends itself to questions, to further research and future discovery. The past life discourses read like synopses of historical novels or sketches of period piece screenplays. Why is such knowledge so rare? If we have lived before, why can't everyone remember their past lives?

The Health Analyses are no less a subject of controversy for some. These health reports give an unprecedented assessment of the mental, emotional, and physical condition. They attest time and again, over and over, that specific ways of thinking produce specific balances or imbalances throughout our being. In essence poor and destructive attitudes produce the appropriate conditions that lead to a malnourished and diseased body. If our way of thinking makes us susceptible to physical disease why can't we all change the way we think and live well past 100?

More and more people believe how they live makes a difference in the condition of their health, their relations with others, and their contentment with their life choices. More and more people seek knowledge to empower them to make these differences. The knowledge offered through School of Metaphysics' readings is presently relevant and personally significant. This knowledge is truthful, insightful, and potentially transforming. Today's uncommon knowledge is tomorrow's revelation.

You are about to meet people from all walks of life who share the questions you have asked yourself: *"Where did I come from?"*, *"Why am I here?"*, and *"Who am I?"* These men and women have found the readings available from the School of Metaphysics to be candid, genuine, and revelatory to their everyday lives. Like the woman whose Health Analysis opened by describing her "attachment to a male form", a male well-known to her who symbolized to her demoralizing competitiveness. Although successful in many areas, the woman discovered many of her health problems were related to misunderstandings she had formed during childhood and continued to perpetuate as an adult. Once she made peace with the male cited in the reading, her mental, emotional, and physical health increased. She had discovered the answer to one of the *why's* in her life.

And the gentleman from Colorado whose father was diagnosed with cancer. Caring a great deal about his father, he offered to arrange for a Health Analysis to be done for him. His father gave his permission but had never really been exposed to anything like this. When the man received the audio recording of the reading, he sat down with his father to listen to it. At the end of the reading, his father looked up at him and said, "There is no way that anyone could know those things about me." The man knew that regardless of what happened with his father's condition, he had given his dad a new way to look at life, a new awareness had been born.

You'll meet the lady from Houston who discovered why her business was slowing and decided to follow the suggestions given during a Business Analysis to work more closely with certain employees while releasing others to rebuild a solid clientele. And the businesswoman from Nashville who discovered she need not sell her business from fear that she and it had achieved its height, but was given clear direction for expansion and increased profits.

You'll come to know the young woman from St. Louis who speaks of an answer to a question that arose when she was fourteen years old. At that time, her grandmother was suffering from Parkinson's disease and very ill. She was hallucinating and talking about things that didn't really happen or people who didn't exist. The woman's family visited her and during the entire conversation the grandmother referred to her son by the name Robert. The man corrected her on several occasions reminding her that his name was Gary, not Robert. Then she took the young woman aside and told her that she had been a good wife to Robert. Like everyone else, the woman reports that she thought grandma was just sick and didn't know what she was saying until years later when she received a Past Life Crossing with her father. The crossing revealed that the woman and her present-day father had indeed been married in a prior lifetime, and his name had been – Robert! This total recall of information was not only pertinent to the woman's present relationship with her father, but also shed new light on her earlier experience with her grandmother.

What you are about to read will astound you.

The ideas will astound you because they make what is beyond the realm of our physical senses understandable and purposeful. The way these ideas have been made to manifest as a service for people from all over the world will astound you for it goes beyond temporal information and recalls knowledge from other times and places. This uncommon knowledge will astound you for it reaches beyond curiosity and momentary self-gratification propelling you into the wealth of wisdom awaiting you in the inner worlds of our existence as individuals and as a human race searching for its spirituality.

— Dr. Barbara Condron

Contents

Part I   The Past Life Readings

Crossing of Paths Readings by Paul Blosser, B.A.

Family Readings by Daniel R. Condron, M.S., D.M.

Part II   The Health Analyses

Part III

Wisdom from those who guide us

Spirit Guide Readings by Barbara Condron, B.J., D.M.

An introduction to

Past Life & Health Readings

I do not know what I may appear to the world.
But, to myself, I seem to have been only
like a boy playing on the seashore,
diverting myself in now and then finding
a smoother pebble or a prettier shell than the ordinary,
whilst the great ocean of truth lay all undiscovered
before me.

—*Sir Isaac Newton, among his last words*

Discovering Uncommon Knowledge

Throughout the history of mankind there have been schools of thought that have taught the development of consciousness throughout the ages. They have been secretive. They have been cloistered in Himalayan monasteries or the halls of the Vatican. They have been specialized as was the school of Pythagorus and Plato's Academy. Such wisdom, the knowledge that is uncommon, has only been available to an elite group, not the masses. You either gained admittance through birth, or through money, or through position, or place on the earth where you were born, or you were appointed to it.

Now, however, because of the education offered by School of Metaphysics anyone has access to uncommon knowledge. You are not appointed for study in this school. You don't have to have a lot of money. You don't have to be born into it. Each individual comes to it and chooses it because his heart leads him here. The student who seeks metaphysical education is a person who questions. He or she seeks answers to the questions that arise in his thinking. He expects that answers exist and that it's not up to some unknown and unseen force or God that those answers are given. Rather he believes, and experience has taught him, that the answers are forthcoming to one who displays the highest abilities known to man – reasoning and intuition. Reasoning is the power in the conscious, waking mind. Intuition is the power in the subconscious, inner mind. Both are a sequence of events in thought. Both can be – and are at SOM – taught and learned.

For a quarter of a century, the School of Metaphysics has provided quality education in the development of consciousness. It is a forerunner in uniting that which very much divides people in the world today. The two groups can most readily be described as people of a religious nature and those of a scientific persuasion. A chasm stands between the two and they seem never to agree. They are constantly at odds. The beauty of metaphysical study, and the application of causal principles, is that it causes the mind to transcend whatever differences or conflicts there might be between science and religion.

We believe, and from our research we know, that you can teach someone how to come into contact with, become familiar with, and access his soul. This has until now been solely religious territory. Science has avoided the issue. For most people the soul is a concept, a result of faith. It's something you believe exists – somewhere. You hope that your soul will be saved from any kind of punishment or purgatory or hell or damnation in the future because you live a good life. This is the extent to which most people go in their thinking. This is the commonly accepted view of the soul.

A metaphysician thinks beyond the norm, embracing bold insights that bring new awarenesses to mankind. Metaphysicians recognize that they are a soul and that the physical body is a temporary form the soul inhabits. They realize the physical conditions of their lives are transient, coming and going in a constant state of change. They only exist in as much as the soul needs to learn. From this vantage point, the physical world becomes the soul's university, offering the opportunity to learn. Learning – or more appropriately understanding – is the sole reason for the soul to assume physical form. It is the height of understanding for someone to identify with the soul, to know what the soul needs, and to be about the work that the soul has to do in order to become whole. The SOM program of study teaches you to access your soul. It teaches you how to develop the discipline required to access the inner levels of your own consciousness. Inner level experience is necessary to know your soul. Inner level experience enables you to see your soul, face to face.

The reading consultations offered as a SOM service are made possible because there are those who have studied, learned, developed, and refined their intuitive abilities. These people access the inner level knowledge for you. They go into the inner levels of consciousness to read the Akashic Records or to read your health aura. Their report of significant past lives or of the wholistic state of your health constitute the reading you receive. You need not have studied yourself to be apprised of knowledge that can bring greater peace of mind and aid you in your soul progression.

The readings are the result of years of experimentation in the use of the inner mind to produce insights into past lifetime existences and states of health. Through years of concentration and meditation practices, individuals have reached deeper and deeper states of consciousness. Lucid dreaming, psi development, intuitive skills, and accumulated wisdom are experienced within these inner levels of awareness. So is memory that extends beyond the boundaries of physical time and reaches into Man's history, collectively and individually. Drawing upon physical memory stored in the brain recalls people, places, and events experienced in the present lifetime. Drawing upon meta-physical memory stored by the soul recalls people, places, and events experienced in previous lifetimes.

It was an effort to use the inner levels to procure knowledge concerning past lives for people other than the person reporting the information that eventually led to the first type of reading, the Past Life Reading. Accessing this information had been so helpful for students it was believed that being able to make such knowledge available to anyone would without question aid in their spiritual unfoldment. The process for reading the past life was repeatedly tested and verified whenever possible. Over several years understanding grew of the process required to garner the information and controls were established to insure the accuracy of what was being perceived and related during a reading.

Although future probabilities were discovered to be information available while functioning in the inner levels of consciousness, early on delving into the future was determined not to be in alignment with the ideal of the School. Therefore our readings do not predict and our Readers are not fortune tellers. Rather Readers are trained to relate only information *significant* to the present lifetime. Because of this profound insights for an individual's growth and soul progression are revealed. This eventually became the Past Life Readings and then the

Past Life Crossings which seek a relevant past lifetime shared by two people. These types of readings continue to relate the information that is most significant, and therefore immediately usable, to the individual(s) requesting the reading. *The Work of the Soul* is a book devoted to past life readings. It includes entire transcripts and commentary by those receiving Past Life, Past Life Crossings, and Family Readings.

Many people find these readings reminiscent of Edgar Cayce's work, a Midwesterner who found he possessed a very real psychic ability which was shared with several hundred people during the early part of the 1900's. It is not chance that during the final quarter of this century, again out of the Midwestern United States, comes a very real psychic ability which has been refined into a skill that can be honed and developed by not just one person, but many. This is in fact the mission of the School of Metaphysics – to respond to what up to this point in history has been in the hands of only a few, revealing what has been kept secret throughout the ages, taught only by small groups ranging from the Freemasons to the Vatican to the Tibetan Buddhist monks and to make that Enlightenment available to anyone who is willing to follow the spiritual disciplines offered.

In addition to the Past Life Readings, the School also offers a Health Analysis. This reading examines the health aura of the individual, relating any mental, emotional, or physical disorder and offering suggestions in each area for wellness and wholeness. The Health Analysis was perfected over several years. From early descriptions relating only the state of the physical body, research expanded to include the emotional influences and eventually the mental causes for physical disorders. In time, the understanding of the specific place in mind to direct the Reader for the attitudinal origin of disorders was discovered and the structure of the Health Analysis was created. Since that time thousands of analyses have been conducted for people to insure good health, as a preventive measure, as a second opinion, and even as a last resort when other health alternatives have failed to identify a problem. The Health Analysis is the subject of the book *First Opinion* published by the School of Metaphysics.

The discovery that readings could be done without the individual being present was made around 1970 when someone who wanted a Past Life Reading intended to be present but found he could not. This opened the door for people anywhere in the world to receive readings. The first readings from outside the United States were for servicemen stationed in the Philippines. Since then readings have been done for people all over the world.

As is true with all of the readings, the other types of readings currently offered through SOM were originally designed in response to individuals' requests for assistance. The Business Analysis was in response to a Kansas City businessman who was familiar with the readings offered to individuals and wanted to know more about his business. The Health Analysis structure lent itself well to examining a body, in this case the business vehicle, and its intelligent director, the owner and employees using that vehicle. A book following business owners who have received several Business Analyses over time is currently being researched and we are seeking a benefactor to fund its publication. It will not only offer a complete picture of how this kind of analysis can save money and increase profits but it will offer invaluable spiritual instruction to help any company to realize the highest expression of the service it wants to provide and accomplish that mission.

In 1980, a woman in Tulsa wanted a reading on her entire family. Through experiments to find the appropriate structure for this type of information, it was discovered that five people in an immediate family usually shared a common past life experience. With six, however, the probabilities started to decline that all members would be in association at another time. Thus the Family Reading was developed. In the mid 70's, a young man from Jamaica wrote to SOM asking for help in finding his accurate birth time and date. This stimulated research into what became the Time of Birth Readings.

Research continues in refining and developing areas to assist others in greater understanding of Self through the service of readings. Currently, research is being conducted in the deepest levels of consciousness. These readings will transcend the soul, going beyond karmic indentures, and revealing the wisdom which wells up from the individual's Spirit. These readings will hopefully enable the recipient to perceive his highest Self, his Atman, his inner Christ consciousness or Buddha consciousness. In this way we hope to accelerate the evolution and Spiritual Enlightenment of everyone on the planet.

Every soul yearns for knowledge that promotes and encourages personal Enlightenment. The School of Metaphysics is dedicated to making this uncommon knowledge available to any seeker. The beauty of the school is that it is designed for those who want to accelerate their evolution. This is really the heart and soul of the School of Metaphysics. It is not so much that what the school has discovered and what it teaches are unique because of lesson content. The Universal Laws and Truths that guide creation can be found in the Holy scriptures of the world. Much of this schooling has been taught in secret schools of thought for centuries or by the great masters throughout history. What is unique is the accessibility of the study and the means to implement it.

The School of Metaphysics is designed to accelerate anyone's evolution, right now. This school exists for the people who are not satisfied with waiting. They are not the kind of person who tends toward procrastination, they do not just wait and see what happens. This knowledge is for the kind of person who wants to make things happen, who has a vision for the future, and an image of what it means to be enlightened. Such a person emulates Great Masters who they have read about, or indeed known, sincerely wanting to be like those people. Such an aspirant desires to be close to his God. He wants to be able to give back to humanity just some of what he has received in lifetime after lifetime after lifetime.

A reading reveals the intentions of the soul and describes the means to fulfill that destiny. A reading enhances Self awareness in an incomparable way. It transforms the recipient's consciousness in direct proportion to her own desire for change and his own willingness to respond. They are at their best revelatory and at their least mind expanding. It has long been my vision that everyone on the planet receive one of these readings. The potential for the resultant elevation of consciousness is awesome. That will be a world I want to see.

The Greatest Investment You Will Make

The School of Metaphysics offers a comprehensive course of study in applied metaphysics. The course is designed to develop the student's awareness and understanding of the three divisions of mind and inner levels of consciousness. At the time I completed the study I didn't see any other place to use my time more productively, both in aiding myself and others, than in my capacity within this organization, the School of Metaphysics. I now spend most of my time teaching and serving in administrative capacities at the international headquarters of the School in Windyville, Missouri, where we receive correspondence and serve people from all over the world each week.

All my life I had attempted to be productive with my life. First it began in physical matters, whether basketball or student body president or Dean's list in college or graduate school. But all those things, after a while, failed to satisfy. With any of the five senses, you can only enjoy so much cake. You can only see so much light until it hurts your eyes. You look at the same landscape and it's beautiful for a while, but if you had to look at it twenty-four hours a day you'd want to see something else. The smell of a rose or even pepper is appealing, but too much of it and you're tired of it or it hurts. Even the desire to touch something or feel something can wane. Grabbing a baseball bat can be fun and enjoyable but if you hold any muscle too long it will begin to atrophy. All of our senses have the capability to give us pleasure, but when they are overused or when you take them to the maximum after a while they fail to satisfy.

If it hasn't already come for you, there will come a time when you've reached the point of appreciating the joy you have in your life, the experiences and whatever satisfaction you've gained through your life, but there is still a desire for something that seems missing. That something is the real Self, the inner Self. It's the you. Where does that real Self exist? It exists in the inner mind. When most people hear the term mind they think of a physical brain, but this is not what I mean by mind. The brain is like a computer. It is an organ of the body as are the heart, the liver, and the lungs. If the brain is an organ similar in function to a computer, what drives it, what directs it? The conscious mind gives the brain commands much like a computer programmer directs a computer's function. What then directs the conscious mind? We can go deeper and deeper into man's existence, to the subconscious levels of mind and the superconscious levels of mind, eventually reaching the point of "I" sometimes called in Eastern literature, the real Self. In the Bible or other Holy Works you may hear it referred to as "I Am". It is the *Self*, the identity and the individuality that is you.

If you've never tried this experiment before, sometime try it. Stop your thoughts and discover what goes on when there is no thought. Find out where you are when there is no thought. Find out what your existence is when there is no thought. If you haven't yet disciplined your mind enough to enter that stage of no thought, then practice it this way, look to see what happens between the thoughts. Look to see who you are or what exists between your thoughts. This is a good experiment and you'll make some productive discoveries. If you desire more control you will pursue a concentration exercise every day, whether you are holding your full attention on a candle, your fingertip, or a dot on the wall. Any stationary object can be the subject of a concentration exercise. In fact, that is how a mantra or a chant, a particular vibration such as Om that you say over and over again, has the same type of effect. The difference with an external object like a candle flame is you are using the sense of sight as the point of focus so your mind can remain still. With the chant or repeated vibration, the sense of hearing is the focal point for the attention.

What do the senses, the attention, the identity and this individuality have to do with reincarnation or past lives? To reincarn, to move from one body, release it, and move into another, you must be doing something in the times between using a physical body. Who is that *you* existing between physical bodies? Where does the Self exist all the time you are in a physical body during a lifetime? Where is the *you* who exists between lifetimes? These are ways to consider the Real You and seek ways to find the Real You.

Reincarnation is similar to the experience of dreaming. You have your waking day's experience, then you go to sleep at night. Where do *you* go? Where does the conscious mind go when you sleep? Perhaps you believe it shuts down. Then, who is in your dream if it is not your conscious mind? When you awake the next morning, perhaps you discount the memory of a dream experience as being meaningless and you get ready to go about your daily physical routine. If you didn't need that dream time, if it wasn't a process of assimilation and preparing for the next day's experience, then all you would do at night would be to lie down and rest your body. Then after one hour or ten hours depending on how hard you worked your body that day, you would be up and ready to go again. You would never need sleep. But there is a need for sleeping time. There is a need for time to harmonize, to process, to integrate, what has been experienced with the waking mind into the inner mind so the two can work together.

Reincarnation is similar because in a sense a whole lifetime is relative to a day in your life. One day is like a mini-incarnation in the sense that you come out into the physical for a day's experiencing then at night you move your attention into the subconscious mind where you assimilate the previous day's learning. At the end of a lifetime, you move your attention into the subconscious mind where again you assimilate the learning gleaned from experiencing. Since a day is twenty-four hours, sixteen or eighteen of which you are awake, it does not take long to assimilate waking experiences, perhaps five, six, eight hours. It takes much less time to assimilate one day's learning than a full lifetime's. As a part of reincarnation, assimilation is the process of coordinating and unifying the connections of experiences during the most recent lifetime with experiences from previous lifetimes. Assimilation is understanding how these experiences relate. A dream works in the same way. You have experiences today and they need to be coordinated with every experience you have had previous to this time.

Why? What would it be like if you went through grade school

and then in seventh grade you studied some subjects that were totally unrelated to anything you had studied before? You would have no point of reference. Schooling is designed with the intention of adding to the material you've already learned. It is the same with a lifetime. You have the opportunity at the end of each lifetime to process the material and learning you've gained and add it to the subconscious mind's storehouse of permanent memory so you can prepare for the next lifetime just as you prepare for the next grade in school.

Some learn a great deal in a lifetime, others less. A lesson can be refused for a whole lifetime. This is similar to grade levels in school. If a student does not learn the material available, then he needs to repeat the opportunity to learn until it is accomplished. Learning is the individual's choice. Why would anyone refuse to learn a lesson? It doesn't seem to make sense, does it? One reason is they do not know how to cause learning. So many times you will hear people say, "why did this happen to me?" or "I don't understand why my life's like it is".

As a Conductor of readings in the School of Metaphysics, I have had the opportunity to meet and serve people from all walks of life and of all nationalities. Many of the questions they ask in Past Life or Health Readings reflect a desire to understand. They want to know why something occurred in their lives or why other experiences tend to recur. In research and study, we have found the point of origin to be some kind of thought process. But most people don't remember their thoughts. They don't remember their thoughts from five or ten minutes ago, let alone yesterday, a week ago, a year ago, or ten years ago. If you consider thought as cause then the physical events in our lives, whether they be our health, job, or personal relationships with friends and family, are a reflection of those thoughts. Memory then becomes very important. If you don't remember your thoughts, how are you going to connect the causal thought with the physical outcome in your life when it arises a week later, six months later, or years later? Usually it doesn't take years for thoughts to manifest, however, if you keep the same thoughts the same situations will continue to occur.

It is vitally important for us to know ourselves. Knowing ourselves begins with remembering and identifying what our thoughts are. Not every single thought needs to be recognized, but rather the repetitive thoughts, the imagined limitations we create in our minds, the habits and compulsions, the way we restrict ourselves, and the way we react to similar situations. Our most beneficial characteristics are also important. We determine what a beneficial characteristic is by the greater fulfillment it produces in our lives, and the good and kindness we do for others. We can call this learning and growth, we can call it greater awareness, we can call it enlightenment, and these characteristics will always add fulfillment to our lives. When there is something missing in life it is time to learn a method to add what is missing.

Each lifetime, the Real You embarks upon a new journey with an express desire, plan, and ideal of gaining an understanding or permanent learning that will contribute to your soul's progression. This ideal is very specific to and for the individual. For one person, the desire may be developing a greater understanding of love; not just the love from a mother to a daughter, a husband to a wife, but an expansion of awareness to include the highest mental and spiritual expressions of love. This is the desire to understand love completely. For another, the ideal might be courage. The courage to stand up to the town bully, or the courage to fight in a war, or the courage to speak before a group of people. There are many expressions of bravery and it can be experienced and understood on every level of consciousness. What is important is knowing what your ideal for this lifetime is, what you most need to build within Self and what steps will build that understanding.

Love, determination, courage, value, authority, dignity, respect, and pride, are some of qualities that we need to develop in order to become whole. Some of them we have already built. Each of us has our own unique set of permanent learning that we've earned. To different degrees each of us is using part of that learning. Maybe you've taken a course in college. You stayed up all night and studied before finals and you got an A in the course. Six months later you don't remember anything you read. You've also passed courses of understandings in past lives. This produced permanent learning that has become a part of permanent memory stored in your soul. You are probably not bringing forth and using all of your understandings this lifetime. By developing *total recall* you can access what is stored in your personal subconscious storehouse.

One of the interpretations of the word *educate* is "to draw forth". This is exactly what happens when there is true learning. When you push yourself beyond previously accepted limitations you can achieve anything you desire. Some people have limitations of age, "I'm too old" or "I'm too young". Others think "I'm the wrong race", "wrong sex", "my hair color's wrong", "I was born in the wrong country", "I was raised in the wrong environment", "I don't have the right education". We can spend our whole life thinking of excuses for why our lives fail to bring fulfillment. What is really important to determine in life is what you want and what you need. This is where trust enters. Trust of your inner voice, for some hear it as an inner voice. For others it is trusting what seems right, a feeling deep in your solar plexus. For others it is following what they know to be the right thing to do.

Sometimes these interests and desires go back to childhood. Sometimes we don't discover a place or a way to use these truths until later in adult life. We find all along we've been preparing to use a lifetime. Anyone who has decided to follow the path of Self development and awareness, one who has chosen the route that will cause the quickest soul evolution and makes that the number one priority in life, will be the one who progresses the fastest. You can focus all of your attention on one physical object, another person, or anything in this wide, beautiful world. If you focus enough attention over time you will achieve what you desire. When you're really honest with yourself and willing to learn from the efforts you make, you will achieve it. The same is true of soul evolution. When you give soul progression your full attention and full energy, then your return will be in that area.

A lifetime is a very short thing when you think about it. I didn't think that fifteen years ago, but one year is only 365 days. You've got 70, 80, 90, or 120 of those years. Make the highest use of the time you have. The degrees I earned from the University of Missouri are in agricultural economics. In economics, one studies benefits and costs. I like to talk about choices and events in terms of the highest return. What is the greatest investment you can make? The investment is *you*, this lifetime. *You* and your 70, 80, or 90 allotted years in this physical body you've chosen. That is your investment. The highest return you can achieve on your investment is a return that will be permanent. Physically we look for permanent or semi-permanent investment such as property. We can put money in the bank or buy stocks and bonds and spread out investments. Many people invest in these areas expecting a return. When you buy a piece of property it is not going to disappear off the face of the earth, it will be there for as long as you own it. Anything you build on that property can last a long time when it is given maintenance and upkeep. Spiritually, the greatest investment is permanent learning, for this is how we invest in the soul. Permanent learning exists beyond the lifetime, indeed forever. The investment in the Self is the greatest investment because it gives the greatest return.

Many people, both contemporary and historical, have believed in reincarnation.   Almost three-quarters of the people living today believe in ideas of reincarnation, but all that kind of information can be readily found in your local library. I accepted the idea of reincarnation because it made sense to me from the first time I heard it while attending college. The part that originally made sense to me was the idea that I am more than a physical body. If I am important and my life has meaning then it must continue having meaning after 70 or more years because this is not a wasteful universe. Man can be wasteful but the universe uses energy completely.

Many people have had psychic experiences. Before I began seriously studying metaphysics, I had psychic experiences that taught me I was not the body. I was sleeping in bed one night and I felt a great vibration which preceded a golden ball of light coming from my chest. The next thing I knew I was up on the ceiling looking down upon my physical body. That was proof for me. You can read about similar experiences such as those who have experienced near-death experiences, or patients under anesthesia on the operating table who watch doctors perform surgery on their bodies and later relate what the doctors were saying when they were believed to be asleep. These kinds of experiences are fairly common where people experience the self as separate from the physical body. For years I have practiced dream interpretation, recording my dreams almost nightly. After a while you begin to realize that in itself is an extrasensory experience. While dreaming you experience a place that is not physical and you are experiencing without use of a physical body. You experience and prove your existence apart from the body every night.

For almost thirty years, the School of Metaphysics has provided over one hundred-thousand readings, many on past lives, for people all over the world. These readings are thrilling because they aid each person receiving the reading to have an instantaneous awareness of who they are like they've never had before. Imagine that you have amnesia. You cannot remember anything that happened before yesterday. You would be functionally impaired. There would be many things you'd be unable to do that you take for granted now. See how limited you would be? Imagine, when you can have the information of who you were before this lifetime, how much more it offers you. A Past Life Reading reveals information about the you you were before this lifetime.

What's the difference between you now and you in the 1700's or 1300's or 2500 B.C.? Two things: one, experience, and two, the degree to which you have used those experiences. If you chose to use your experiences for progression you are significantly different. You have probably many times watched two people experience the same situation. One gets mad, the other one breaks out in laughter. Each reacts according to their unique experiences, and the difference shows in how experiences have been used to build security in the Self. For the one who lacks security, a situation will arise threatening the security, and the person will feel the need to protect the Self becoming angry. For the confident person, an opportunity will arise and inner security will provide an objectivity enabling them to keep the situation in perspective and even find humor in it. Each lifetime we have the opportunity to create learning for ourselves. We also have the right to choose how much learning we will create. You don't have to wait five lifetimes to reach the level of awareness you desire. You can quicken your soul growth or spiritual development. It's important to trust yourself.

Past Life Readings are like evolutionary vitamins. Today we take vitamins when food fails to provide the value the body needs. A Past Life Reading gives you instantly something your mind can use that it needs. The conscious mind and physical body did not know how to find the answers that the past lifetime offers you immediately. The first time I received a Past Life Reading I knew I'd received in ten minutes more knowledge about me than I had gained in the entire preceding year. It wasn't magic. It was no more magic than you turning on the television and watching a report on what happened in China or Russia or Brazil or Canada. Yet, a hundred years ago you'd probably be doing pretty well to hear of world events at all unless you happened to be a sailor who traveled around the globe. Television provides an increase in the efficiency of communication. An idea or image originates at one point on the globe and can move almost instantaneously to you, the receiver, located at another point on the globe. This is exactly what Past Life Readings do. They retrieve or collect information from one place that you do not have access to normally, and present it to you. The great thing about the reading is that all the information is about *you*! That really is the most valuable information there is.

I love history because history tells me where we have been. It tells me where we came from. Perhaps you think, "History's not about me, I'm here right now." It was *you* existing in a different physical body and living what we now see as history. The more you can know about your Self the better. The first key to change is self knowledge. When I say change I mean it in a positive sense. Many view change negatively. A hurricane hits the coast of Florida, killing hundreds and destroying thousands of homes. That's change, change is bad. However, change does not mean destroying something, rather change is creation. When new houses are being built, that's change. Change is accepting what is in your environment, creating something better, and in the process bettering you.

Each one of you is vitally important. You are vitally important because you are a soul, a spark from the Creator. You are vitally important because you are *I AM*. You are also vitally important because every step up the soul ladder of evolution you make places you in a much greater position to aid others. You never know when one kind word offered from your value and wisdom may go all the way around the world and come back again. You can affect that many people beneficially, that's how important you are. If you've not accepted it to this point, it is time to accept your importance. To accomplish something greater than what you are, to accomplish something beyond what you have created already, requires something that is always available and that is imagination. Unfortunately, not enough people practice using it, but fortunately more and more people are beginning to use imagination. You can call it visualization or creative mind, but it is the image-maker, the ability of the mind to form images. For you to create anything with intention, it is required that you first have a mental image. If you were to go from where you are to Cairo and you had no mental image, no map, you could go north or south or east or west and you wouldn't know how far to go. Without a mental image you wouldn't even know if you had passed it already. It would take you forever to get there! With a mental image, or in this case a map, someone giving you directions, or memory of having been to Cairo before, you can go directly where you desire.

A Past Life Reading serves as part of that mental image road map because it gives you a snapshot of one section of who you are. This kind of reading gives the past lifetime that is most significant to the present; one of your past lives out of all the many that is relative to you right now. What makes that lifetime significant is not a "what" but *who*. You make it significant by your particular set of situations and circumstances and most importantly the attitudes that you hold. For instance, the most important thought you hold in mind can be positive or negative. It can be love or hate, will power or passivity, these are just extremes of a quality you were attempting to develop in a past lifetime and left incomplete. You started to pursue that quality, did some activity toward and gained some learning of it, but you did not complete that area of your learning. Now this lifetime you are fortunate. You have created situations and opportunities to complete that area of your learning. The Past Life Reading will reveal what was left unfulfilled in a previous life and give significant insights for fulfillment in your present life.

Look at your life. You will see that anytime you had a goal that matched your desire, you first had an idea born from your desire to experience something. You earned your ideal through action, putting forth the effort necessary by making changes in your Self. And you were fulfilled. In fact, you were not only fulfilled when you achieved the goal, but you were gaining joy and enthusiasm for living life all along the way because it was your special goal and sacred desire. You knew it was what you wanted to do. You can share that awareness with people all through your life because it has value and benefit.

It is very satisfying for me to be able to offer the readings to people. To see the look of realization on a person's face, to recognize the joy at finding an answer to a question that has been bothering someone a long time, or to see the fulfillment of learning something about Self, that's worth more than any amount of money. It is about the happiest feeling and experience anyone can have. Maybe you know of someone who has saved another's life. Maybe you have had this experience yourself. You can imagine or remember the joy experienced from this noble act. The Past Life Reading offers insight and truth to the person requesting it which can contribute to a greater life than he or she has now.

There is nothing more important than realizing *who* you are. It is important that you decide the quickest, fastest way to achieve that Self awareness and Self knowledge and pursue it. By opening the doors of permanent memory you begin your journey toward *total recall* and give yourself the wealth of what you have already attained. Command of memory spurs the imagination to *become* and evolution is quickened. What you add to yourself will last for an eternity.

Dr. Daniel R. Condron

Part I
The Past Life Readings

What people tell us.....concerning Past Life Readings...

"I would like to express my profound thanks to you for the Past Life Reading I have just received. The insight and advice you have given me regarding my way of life are most valuable and highly appreciated. I shall certainly act on them." — Kevin Lees, Terang, Vic, Australia

"Just wanted to give you some feedback on the past life reading I received from you. The life described is almost a duplicate of my present one! I have as hobbies all the things I was taught in that life. I can sew and embroider darn near anything! Also, I studied painting privately for 18 years and music (piano & organ) for nine years. The desire to be a music composer in that life also makes sense. Although I am not involved in a musical career there are many things about music (for which I have a passion!) that I simply 'know'. I frequently find myself rearranging melodies I hear on the radio to make them more beautiful!

Also I once again chose marriage and family over a career because it was 'expected' of me...In this life I am of Italian descent and marriage and family are very important to us –I have though now taken steps to fulfill some of those unresolved desires. I have not the time to go into how relevant the instructions given to not blame others and trust the creative powers of my inner mind were. In fact, that section of the tape reduced me to tears!

I do hope that sometime next year I will be able to pursue studies with your school..." —Dorothy McDermott, Belle Mead, New Jersey

"I have been a student of Edgar Cayce's readings for some years and always thought how incredibly helpful it would be to find and follow one's true path if there were more 'Cayces' on this planet today, to continue to help lift the veil that hangs between ourselves and this greater wisdom. Thank you for the work that you in SOM are doing. This world is in such need for the vision and selfless service that you all provide." — Gert Basson, Santa Monica, California

"I recently had a past life crossing done and it was quite a remarkable experience. My friend and I wondered about the outcome, but when we heard the reading we were hardly surprised at the nature of the relationship it portrayed. For me it made such complete sense and gave me a sense of incredible calm. Hernan was amazed at the similarities not only between he and I then and now but because the woman your reader described as me, the mother of Hernan, and all the circumstances involving conception, birth, health, life, etc. are identical to his mother now."

— Patricia Korval, Brooklyn, New York

"Several years ago someone with your organization did a reading regarding a past life crossing with an individual. The reading was hard to believe immediately but over time proved to be remarkably accurate. I wonder if you could do another past life crossing for me with another individual."

— Marta Been, Boulder, Colorado

Significant Past Lives

Since Man developed the ability to reason, he has searched for answers to questions that could only be conceived by an inquisitive, creative mind. For thousands of years, many have become content to meekly accept the beliefs of someone in a position of authority. Upon receiving answers to some of their questions, other queries remain unasked by a mind that agrees to only follow the leader. In this way, Man's inherent urge to create and evolve is stifled, his mind entrapped in physical identity and his thoughts the victim of imagined limitation.

Yet, throughout history there have always existed those individuals who continue to exercise the mind's thinking abilities. These people build their identity as creative beings and form their thoughts as answers to the questions from Self and humanity. Self reliant, they are not too proud to embrace the thinking and experience of others that will accelerate their own quest toward enlightenment.

You have heard of these individuals before. They are history's heroes and heroines. They are the philosophers who mastered the law of relativity. They are the scientists who mastered the law of cause and effect. They are the inventors and artists who mastered the laws of creation. They are the kings and queens who mastered the laws of divine birthright. They are the Spiritual leaders who mastered the law of existence. Each of these is an individual like you and me. Individuals possessing the same universal structure of mind and functioning within the same Universal Laws that we do today. Each of these individuals used the mind to be a whole, functioning Self.

The inquiring mind wonders what separates history's heroes and heroines from the average, normal, and common man. The answer is found through study, application, and understanding of the nature and purpose for our existence.

Metaphysics is the scientific pursuit of mastering the mind's creative ability. In Greek *meta* means "beyond, with, after... change" and *physikos* means "pertaining to nature, to bring forth...to be". The classical definition of metaphysics is *that science which seeks to trace the branches of human knowledge to their first principles in the constitution of our nature, or to find what is the nature of the human mind and its relations to the external world.* In the past decades, investigation by instructors and students in the School of Metaphysics has led to identifying and harnessing uses of three principles of mind. These principles are known as Creative Mind, Prana, and Akasha.

Creative Mind lends its intelligence to mind through the faculties of memory and imagination. The ability to move and transform is found in the principle of prana, or energy as it is utilized by the individual's will. The use of these principles acts upon akasha, the mind substance of our existence as thinkers, to shape, mold and form our desires and intentions into the situations and circumstances of our lives.

Commanding these three principles gives rise to direct experience and knowledge of Self beyond our conscious, waking existence in the physical level of consciousness. This developed perception enables us to exist in the inner planes of the subconscious mind and bring back with us full recall of our experiences, similar to an individual's ability to remember dream experiences. As time is invested in education and practice, a disciplined student can develop skills in using the three principles of mind and gain access to the truth and wisdom stored in his subconscious mind.

The subconscious mind of each individual, many times referred to as the soul, holds all understandings that have been earned. For this reason, your subconscious mind only knows truth. Your subconscious mind provides a place where your evolution as a thinker is permanently recorded.

The subconscious mind of Man can be likened to a puzzle. The outlining form of the puzzle becomes the guideline used to enter puzzle pieces. This outline is stored in the soul as a reflection of the blueprint

for your maturation as a Thinker. As the cause of ea
physical life is identified, understood, and made a
discover a piece of your puzzle that will fit into the outh.
need for incarning into physical life will continue until
completed.

At this stage of Man's evolution most of the puz_ie can be
perceived, thus we find talents and abilities that we did not learn in this
lifetime making themselves known. As you use what you have already
made a part of your Self, you accelerate the addition of more puzzle
pieces to the puzzle that is your soul.

To insure that evolution toward maturity of the Thinker continues, the Universal Law of Cause and Effect operates in our lives as what
is known as karma. *Karma* is a Sanskrit word meaning *act* or *fate–that
which has been spoken.* To have the ability to know what your karmic
obligations are and to add understanding of these to your Self, is to cause
the completion of your soul's puzzle.

It is with these truths in mind that the Past Life Readings,
Crossing of Paths Readings, and Family Readings are provided for
individuals requesting insight into their present lifetime. Through a
trained and developed use of the subconscious mind, Conductors and
Readers work as a team to identify the causes for present day situations
and circumstances in your life. Readers are skilled in reporting events
recorded in mind substance so this information can be made available
to aid you in identifying the needs of your soul.   For this reason, each
of these types of readings reveals the karmic obligations of the individuals involved.

Readers are also adept in describing what is perceived that will
accelerate the understanding necessary to relieve karmic obligations. In
readings given through the School of Metaphysics, this information is
found in the significance of the past lifetime related to the present
lifetime.

To obtain this kind of information, the Conductor directs the
Reader's attention to a specific place in the subconscious mind. This
place exists only in mind and is known as the point between the fourth
and fifth levels of consciousness. The Akashic Records are found here
because this place is the end of mental consciousness and the beginning
of physical consciousness within mind. Once access to the Records is

...red, the Reader traces the individual's desire for the information requested through the use of his name. The process would be similar to using the title and author of a book to search and find information in a library. Once you've gained the skill of using the library, any information stored there is open to your use.

For more than two decades, thousands of people have used information revealed from the Records to enrich their lives. In this section, faculty of the School of Metaphysics share their own and others' experiences with these types of readings. Pam Blosser introduces you to the continuity of existence beyond the physical by describing the Past Life Readings, Paul Blosser explores the nature of our relationships with others in Past Life Crossing of Paths, and Dr. Daniel Condron gives insight to the karmic obligations found in familial choices in Family Readings.

If this is your first introduction to the readings provided by the School of Metaphysics, you will discover many new worlds are open to you. If you have already availed yourself of this service, you will learn new ways to use the information gained, enhancing your quest to become a whole, functioning Self.

*"It is no more surprising
to be born twice than once,
everything in nature is resurrection."*
—*Voltaire (1700's)*

Past Life Readings
by Pam Blosser, B.A., D.M.

Questions from an Open Mind

Where do I come from? Why am I here? Where am I going? These age-old questions are the link to the deepest yearnings in Man. There is an order to the universe and the surrounding world. There is purpose to life and an order to its seemingly disjointed string of events. Why? Why? The urge to understand and know Truth propels the reasoner to search for answers extensively both inwardly and outwardly.

I, too, have asked the question why. While living in London and taking a year-long intensive course in the Maria Montessori Method of Education I asked myself this question. While I was there, I met a young street poet named Peter. Peter had a collection of folk instruments among which was a beautifully handcrafted folk harp called a clarsech. I enjoyed spending time at Peter's flat working on assignments for my education course. We both enjoyed the freedom of going about our own business knowing that there was someone close by but without feeling obligated to entertain each other or getting distracted from our own goals.

One evening I was at Peter's apartment working on my projects. Now Peter was an avid soccer fan and this particular evening he announced he would be going down the street to watch a soccer game.

I told him I would like to study in his living room while he was gone. I usually studied in a small room off the living room, but thought I would enjoy the change of scenery since the rest of the apartment would be empty. He said fine and in a short time was out the door.

The living room was where Peter kept his folk instruments. It was distracting to sit in the room with them, especially the beautiful harp. It rested in a dark corner of the room quiet yet alive with music ringing within its dark wooden frame. I looked up periodically at the harp as I worked, my attention moving back and forth from my notebook to the harp in the corner. It silently beckoned me to its side to touch its dark, wooden frame and stroke its silken strings.

Finally I laid my papers aside and approached the beautiful instrument. Sitting down behind it I pulled its wooden frame back against my right shoulder and lightly plucked its strings. How wonderful! Each touch was music! The progression of sounds made a tune and the accompanying strings wove a harmony around the melody line. As I played, my only thought was to discover how many tunes I could create. I looked up at the clock and to my surprise forty-five minutes had passed. I could hardly wait for Peter to return.

When he walked in the door I excitedly related to him what I had experienced. "I have to have a harp to take back to the States with me!" I exclaimed.

Within a few days Peter had located a harp maker who lived on the south side of London, the other side of London from where I lived. Together we went to his shop where I purchased a harp to take back to the United States. I loved my harp immediately as if it were a long lost friend. It seemed so delicate and vulnerable as I carried it back all the way across London. I had to transfer several times on the subways and buses to make the connections. How weary I was as we arrived at Peter's flat.

I wondered how I was going to get my harp back to the States. I would just have to take it on the plane as carry-on luggage. When I got to the airport I was told the harp was too big and I would have to check it as luggage. I worried about the harp all the way across the Atlantic Ocean like a mother worrying about her child on her first day of school.

When I was settled back home, I began to compose and arrange music on my harp. I did this by ear – something I had never done before.

The music I created was unique, in a category by itself. My music was haunting, sometimes lush. The chord progressions I chose seemed almost otherworldly.

At that time I knew little about past lives but I asked, "Why?" Why was there a strange and comfortable familiarity with this instrument? Why did it seem so easy to arrange and compose music on it? Why was it that the music that came so easily seemed so different from any other music I had heard before?

Answers from Unexpected Places

Shortly after I returned to the United States I took a job teaching in a Montessori School. I also came across a brochure about the School of Metaphysics. I was looking for spiritual discipline. The brochure outlined such areas as concentration, meditation, healing, the power of the mind and Past Life Readings from the akashic level. Much of what I read made sense but the Past Life Readings left me cold.

First of all, reincarnation was something that I hadn't seriously considered and I had never heard of the akashic level before. I called and talked to the director of the school, asking her several questions about the classes and services offered by the school. One of these questions was about the Akashic Records.

She explained to me that the Akashic Records was a "place" within the inner levels of mind where everything that had ever been thought, said, or done in the physical world was recorded. To me, it was like a twilight zone between the spiritual and physical realms and this was where the information for Past Life Readings was stored. Anyone knowing the right steps could tap into and draw out the information much like keying into a computer and requesting information to come forward. It all sounded pretty far out to me and I told her so.

She invited me to an open discussion coming up a few nights later and I decided to go. The topic was on psychic happenings, another area that seemed far out to me. What impressed me that evening were the people at the center; down-to-earth, straightforward, practical minded and most of all, relaxed. When I left that night I felt more peaceful than I had felt for a long time. I wanted to learn how to have

ɔf peace too. I immediately enrolled in the classes, beginning
ᵣ......ᵤl discipline that would aid me in building the peace of mind
I wanted to attain.

The classes revolved around practical skills of the mind so very
little was mentioned about reincarnation, Past Life Readings, or the
Akashic Records until it came time for my class reading after Lesson
Eight. The student who at this point in the lessons has developed a
certain amount of understanding through the mental exercises can
respond to the information in the reading and make some productive
changes. One afternoon, Brad, one of the school's teachers, approached
me about my class reading. Lamely I muttered, "I don't think I'm ready
for it."

Brad laughed and exclaimed, "Now I've heard everything."
With that remark I knew I was going to get my reading whether I wanted
it or not, no matter what kind of excuse I could find. I had come to know
that the teachers at the school would support me in my strengths but
definitely not in my fears. I was resigned to the idea but reassured
myself that I didn't have to believe in reincarnation as a result.

The day of my class reading arrived. I was met by my teacher,
Merala Heins, as I entered the school. We chatted for a few moments
in the kitchen and then a rather large man with a goatee sauntered into
the room. My teacher introduced him as Dr. Jerry Rothermel, president
of the School of Metaphysics. He announced that it wouldn't be long
before we would be starting.

I walked into the living room. Seated on the couch was a
delicate looking young woman, her blonde hair pulled back in a bun at
the nape of her neck. She had settled in the middle of the couch, her
hands relaxed in her lap, her eyes closed. Dr. Rothermel seated himself
to her left. After speaking to her softly for a few minutes he said:

> *"You will search for the identity of the entity referred to as
> Pamela Elizabeth Stewart. You will relate a significant
> incarnation for this entity."*

The Reader began speaking.

> *"This one is seen as female form. We see this to have been*

in an area now known as England. We see that this one had accepted a position at a very young age as that of governess and that this one would be taking care of another's children. We see that this one began to use much of this one's creativity and imagination, and began to establish many of the educational outlets for these children. We see that this was very impressive to the parents of the children, as well as to the others who saw the results of this. We see that there were contacts made in which this one was allowed a great amount of education but most of this was in a teaching capacity. We see that eventually this one was very much involved with the higher education of this time period. We see that this one dealt with many subjects for every day there was a need to create an interest in a particular subject which this one would use. We see that this was due to the creativity and the enthusiasm with which this one taught. We see also that there was a great ability which this one developed in relating what was in the knowledge to that of the physical life of the students, which made the subjects much more real and the students much more interested in the studies."

I had never met this Reader before. Yet she could "see" attributes about me that made so much sense and fit so well. In the present lifetime, I had taught a variety of subjects from cooking to swimming to English as a second language. Teaching had always come easily for me no matter what the subject. There was no way she could have known about me. I had not mentioned to my teacher or anyone at the school the many subjects I had taught during my life. Following the description of the past lifetime, the Reader offered how this information was significant to my life at this time.

"In the present time period there is a great need in regards to the many abilities which this one has. We see that there has not been a connection made within this one's life at the present time to see the abilities and to see them in action and the results which they will incur. We see that there is a great creativity which this one applies quite accurately to the physical. We see however that this understanding has not been brought to this one's attention and there has been an

> *attitude established upon this one's part that self is starting*
> *from the very beginning. Would suggest to this one however*
> *that there is much knowledge to be drawn on of a practical*
> *nature as well as of an abstract nature in this one's previous*
> *understanding. Would suggest to this one that the purpose*
> *of the present time period for this one is not just to take*
> *information or to take from the situations on how to learn or*
> *how to apply the teaching concepts but there is much that this*
> *one has to give also and it is time, in order for this one to*
> *fulfill this purpose, to put this into activity. This is all." (9-*
> *29-77-1-CK)*

The reading fit so well with my new job at the Montessori school. In spite of all the experience I had had in my life, teaching at the Montessori school seemed brand new. It seemed I had much to learn. What if I had actually been this teacher? If so, I knew more about teaching than I was giving myself credit. I could stop being so nervous about not knowing enough and trust my intuition about teaching.

After hearing the reading it was no longer important to argue about reincarnation as a fact. Arguing about the existence of reincarnation seemed like an intellectual mind game much like arguing about how many angels could dance on the head of a pin. It seemed trivial in comparison to the importance of using each day of life. What I learned from that reading in regards to reincarnation was the importance of time.

Each day – even each moment – is like a reincarnation. This moment is affected by how you've used the ones previous to it. How you use the present moment will have its effect on the ones to come. What you do with each moment of your life is important. You choose whether you're going to learn and change or do the same thing you've always done. With the first choice there is growth; with the second, limitation and stagnation.

Within your daily activities if you make a mistake you have the opportunity to correct it. If you're practicing a sport or a song on the piano you can practice it again until you become proficient at it. Your imagination is your resource to improve the quality of these attributes. If you don't like what you did yesterday you can do something different today. If you did like what you did yesterday you can do it again today and possibly reach a greater depth of understanding with it. Each day you can find out just how strong or courageous or tolerant or patient or persistent you have become. These individual choices determine how full of learning and growth your life is. And isn't this what life is all about? You are here to learn who you are as creators, what kind of creator you are and what kind of creator you can be.

The more I explored reincarnation as a day-to-day physical progression of learning, the more sense it made to me to apply this principle to its spiritual level. Each lifetime, as you learn through your physical experiences, you, as a soul, can add to your identity of who you are as a creator. You can discover just what you're made of as you face and respond to life. You can identify the height of integrity to which you are reaching, and you can admit as you experience what you create what kind of mental creator you are.

Assignments from the Soul

Just like you have the memory in your brain of the yesterdays leading to today, you also have a sense of the continuity of the steps in your learning from lifetime to lifetime. This is stored in the permanent memory of your soul called the subconscious mind. Most of you, however, are not consciously aware of the steps you have taken as a soul that have brought you where you are now in your own evolution. Most of you have forgotten how to access the information in the Akashic Record, the holder of your soul's past. Nor do you remember how to access your own subconscious mind, the holder of your understandings. These understandings are qualities such as courage, compassion, self-value and a sense of order, to name a few, that you have built through repeated purposeful action in previous lifetimes. They are now a permanent part of your identity.

You might think of your mind as a giant iceberg. Only the top of the iceberg appears above the surface of the water. This is the part of yourself that you can experience with your five senses. It is called your conscious mind, your physical body, and to some extent your emotions. Now look below the surface of the water and what do you see? The majority of the iceberg exists below the water's surface just as the majority of yourself exists "below" the surface of your own conscious existence. This vastness is your soul, your spirit, your essence. If you identify with the physical body only it would be like thinking that the tip of the iceberg is all of you that exists. What is real is only what the iceberg can see, feel, hear, taste, and smell. You as the tip of the iceberg identifies as incomplete and separate. The quest to understand who you are is to identify with the whole and reunite the iceberg once again.

Each lifetime you have the opportunity to explore a chosen facet of yourself to be united with it, or to make it part of your identity. In the beginning of evolution this completeness was more like a blueprint of your potential than the finished product. It takes the soul and the physical conscious identity working together to identify each part of the blueprint and then actualize it.

The actualization process begins with a belief – a belief that you are strong or organized in your thinking, for example. It is a belief in yourself that you can create something valuable in your life. By applying this belief in your daily life you have an experience that calls for the quality you believe you have. You discover just how strong or organized you really are. Then it becomes a knowing. You know through the experience that you are as strong, stronger or not as strong as you believed you were. If you believe you can be stronger you begin to imagine what you would do differently the next time a similar experience occurs in your life. This reasoning process gives you a place to grow and expand your identity toward your real potential. Each time you respond to a belief that you are valuable to humanity you are setting up a condition to learn something about yourself and unfold your identity – fulfill the blueprint, as it were. Evolution is this process of unfolding.

The soul needs the physical self in this process because knowing comes only through purposeful experience. These experiences do not "happen haphazardly". They are caused intentionally by yourself out of a need to identify and understand. Now this Self I am referring to is not the self that can be tasted, touched, seen, heard, or smelled. I'm not talking about the tip of the iceberg. I'm talking about your soul. Your soul knows what parts of the blueprint have been fulfilled and what parts are yet to be fulfilled. Your soul perceives the physical experiences as the means to fulfill this blueprint. Your soul draws you, the outer self, "mysteriously" to these places of learning. And your soul receives the understanding from the experience into itself as a permanent part of your identity. The outer self feeds the soul by learning from experiences.

Each lifetime it is the soul that chooses what physical conditions will offer the best opportunities to begin the learning process for that lifetime. Then it is up to the outer self to cooperate with this learning process by the choices it makes. How well are you living up to the learning your soul or inner Self has assigned to your physical or outer self? As the following excerpt reveals, fulfilling the soul's assignment is the key to happiness in our present life.

> *"We see at present time within this one there is a love that this one does have for structure and discipline. We see at those times when this one is devoting the mind and devoting the Self to some form of discipline that this one is very content, for this one does reach greater understandings and does produce what this one desires in her life. We see however there are times when this one does scatter the attention and does not pursue what is true to this one's desires and at those times when this one is turning away from what this one truly desires, this one does become very unhappy."* (7-26-90-10-LJF)

When information concerning past lives is made known, you can enhance your ability to define who you are by adding to what has already been built within the Self. Notice how in the following reading examples there was a quality gained in a past life now being added to in this lifetime. The first is of a female who in a past life was raised in a poor family in the Middle East. There was much love in this family. She was taught as she grew up that she was beautiful, she had much love and she would always find blessings in whatever experiences were in her life. She perceived her hard work as a labor of love and a giving to God. She knew she would be rewarded in the afterlife. She was seen by others in her community as a source of freshness and joy and she passed these ideals on to her children. In that lifetime she learned about loving and giving unconditionally.

In this lifetime she is adding to this understanding because she is discovering that although she wants to give, there are those who do not want to receive from her. She is learning she need not gauge the value of her love by how others wish to receive. Rather her lesson is to continue to give freely, respecting those who do not wish to receive and seeking out those who are receptive to her love.

The second example comes from a reading of a female who lived a past life in Italy in the 1500's. In this past life she used music as a way to draw her family together during times of hardship and conflict. She took a deep responsibility for the harmony in the family and in so doing became personally involved with their lives. She developed a great knack for listening and offering counsel to others.

In this lifetime she possesses a concern for other people and uses the listening and counseling skills developed in that lifetime. She is learning to relate what she gives to others to her own growth.

> *"Would suggest that to cause there to be growth and awareness in the Self is to cause there to be an elevation of this one's availability and this one's service that can be given to other people." (9-28-90-1-BGO)*

These are two good examples of how we can add to both our learning and identity from one lifetime to the next.

Reading the Records

A Past Life Reading is a valuable resource of information. In the School of Metaphysics, as part of the course work in the advanced series, students are given the keys to going into the subconscious mind at will, tapping into the Akashic Record and drawing forth desired information about their own past lives or the past lives of others. This information is also made available to anyone who desires it through the service of a Past Life Reading given by a trained Reader and Conductor.

The past life brought forth in a Past Life Reading is one significant to the needs of the person requesting it. The reading reveals information about a past life that relates to the present conditions and circumstances of that individual. This type of reading addresses the question: what thoughts are affecting current conditions in relation to the process of learning and soul growth. Was there a quality developed such as courage or compassion that could be drawn on now or developed further? A female who was a healer in China in the 1200's is now being told to evaluate the abilities and talents from previous lifetimes so she can offer them to others. Another female who learned about self-control, self-discipline, maintaining a sense of peace and calm, and of identifying her own source of being in her lifetime in China in 500 A.D., is now being told to use that self-control and self-discipline in order to learn to focus on the quality of serenity.

Was there learning avoided in a past life that now is being faced again? A Past Life Reading offers much more than a means to satisfy curiosity or inflate the ego. It serves to stimulate the ego to act from the perspective of the information revealed.

In a past life, a female was born into a family in Italy in the 1700's. Her brothers and sisters were quite a bit older so she was raised like an only child. During that lifetime she was very creative in the fields of singing, dance, drawing and painting. She spent much time alone pursuing these interests and isolating herself from others. In this lifetime she once again deals with a sense of isolation in her need to associate with others. It was suggested that:

> *"In order for this one to understand and to love this one's own self and to create the identity that this one wants this will involve association with others for it is in association with others that this one does truly understand what this one has to give and what causes this one to be unique." (7-25-90-9-LJF)*

Because the Past Life Readings relate to the present situations in a person's life it relates to the karma of the individual. Karma is a Sanskrit word meaning "to do" or action. Karma relates to the cause and effect action of the universe. This means any action will produce certain results. The action referred to here is not just physical action but more significantly mental action or intention. To illustrate, here are two situations. In the first Joe is gagging on some food and John wants to save him. He administers the Heimlich maneuver to unlodge the food in his throat. In the second situation John is angry at Joe and wants to hurt him. He comes up behind him and grabs him in the middle to knock the breath out of him. The physical action is the same but the mental action is different. In the first situation John wants to help Joe; in the second, he wants to hurt him. The mental action or intention is what causes the karma and it is relieved through understanding.

Karma is an educative process. It is one of the best methods you have of gauging where you are in your spiritual growth. Here is an example of how karma works in a physical sense. Let's say you are going to bake a cake and you know how much flour, sugar, eggs, baking powder, and vanilla to add but you don't know how much salt to add. You add the salt you think will work. When you eat the cake you find it needs more salt. You have just experienced karma because you have experienced the results of what you caused. You recognize the amount of salt is out of balance with the other ingredients. The next time you make a cake you have the opportunity to correct the amount of salt. When you have learned the right amount of salt to add to the cake, by again experiencing what you cause, you have relieved your karma. The amount of salt is in proportion or in balance with the other ingredients in the cake and you can reproduce a delicious cake every time.

Here is an example of karma in a reading where the individual is learning about being true to inner desires. The individual, a female in this lifetime, was a male in New England. Her name in that lifetime was Benjamin Edward Montague. As a young boy he experienced love and concern from his parents which gave him a sense of security. However, his parents sent him away to a boarding school because it offered him a greater education than the school in the area where he lived. The teachers within this school emphasized discipline but without a sense of love or concern. Benjamin had difficulty learning under these conditions. He counted the days when the school year would end so he could return home.

His parents would not listen to his desires to change schools and Benjamin was afraid to be too insistent or to voice his desires. Benjamin responded to this condition by establishing the attitude of life being hard and having to fight to enjoy or really use a situation. On top of this Benjamin became a lawyer, a profession he cared very little about. He would much rather have been a doctor or veterinarian. He did well at his profession even though he found the work boring and did not care to be around the criminal element.

> *"We see that this one built understandings of consistency and follow through on just about whatever he decided to do. We see that this one did also build an understanding of love in this one's family but this did not extend to the rest of the life."*

The karma that was left unfulfilled dealt with learning the difference between unselfishness in giving and sacrifice.

> *"We see in the present time that this one has difficulty making choices in the life direction that are based around this one's own fulfillment or the meeting of this one's needs. We see that this one makes choices where this one puts the self in very difficult situations and does not know why other than this one thinks this is what this one should do. We see that there is a need to recognize that when the greatest love does occur within this one is when this one makes the choices in this one's life based upon this one's desires and fulfilling those desires. It is important for this one to learn the difference between this one fulfilling this one's desires and falling into a rut of selfishness that causes stagnation, for distinguishing this is important for this one's development of this one's own trust and to really live the life fully and as respectfully as this one needs to do."* (6-16-90-3-CSR)

What this individual realized from the reading was to pursue desires, to trust the inner authority and feel comfortable with it. To fulfill the inner desires, serving other people is necessary so that both the Self and others benefit. This was the "missing link" in understanding that could now be applied. Real change or understanding comes through experience and practice.

Paying Karmic Debts

Although karmic experiences most often involve other people the karmic debt is always to yourself. Remember it is the intention behind the action that actually sets up the karma. That intention is yours and no one else's. No one "does anything to you". They do stimulate and influence you, but you have the free will to respond to their influence in whatever manner you choose. In one reading it was suggested that:

> *"When this one does experience reactions to others in this one's environment that this one identify what ways of thinking or acting are stimulating this one's anger or other reactions. For we do see that these others are mirrors for this one of qualities that are out of balance within this one's own Self. Would suggest from this point that this one then determine how this one would want to cause these to change." (1-16-91-8-LJF)*

It is through coming to terms with your attitude and changing your response, until it is comfortable, to one producing growth that you are able to pay off this debt. When asked about karma with other people in a reading, the Reader replied:

> *"Would suggest to this one that in terms of this one's indebtedness, that this is in regards to her own growth and development. The response to the roles that other people play are according to this one's choices and that of others in terms of accelerating or retarding this one's growth and progression." (9-9-90-3-BGO)*

Through your own choices you can actually speed up or slow down your soul growth. The best way to speed up soul growth is in giving. The best way to slow down soul growth is in holding back from giving. Here is an example of how an individual's dream was dashed in a former life and how he holds back from giving this lifetime. The reading revealed that in the previous life the man had been an architect in England. He had a dream to build a decorative and powerful sculpture to be placed at the gate of his city and provide inspiration to those who passed. So precious and valuable was this dream that he was overly hesitant to communicate it to others for fear of being ridiculed. Yet this dream continued to be a driving force within him.

Eventually he met a wealthy man to whom he revealed his secret dream. This man supported him so much that he became his benefactor and agreed to front the cost of the building of this structure.

The architect drew up the plans for the statue. Builders were sought out and contracted. But even as beautiful as the structure was and with the full support and respect of the benefactor, the builders thought it was a waste of time, money, and resources. Their opposition stopped the construction from taking place. The man's fear of his most precious dream being rejected had in fact come to pass. He was so disappointed he felt he had no reason to continue living. As a result his liver began to degenerate and after a time he died of a liver disease.

From this past life, the karma that still needs to be brought into balance or understood is the sense of vulnerability that ideas or dreams can be invalidated by what other people think or say.

> *"We see within this one there are great dreams and ideals that this one holds within the self and these give this one much drive and enthusiasm in this one's daily life. We see once again for this one to be very closed in this one's communication for this one is always afraid someone will take away from this one's self what this one does think and what this one holds dear to the Self. Would suggest to this one for this one to be very visionary, very clear and very brilliant in the expression of this one's thoughts. We do see this one to have much ability to be charismatic. Would suggest for this one to bring these visions closer to home by incorporating the idea that the individuals that are in this one's life at the present period of time are those who are compatible with this one's desires. Would suggest to this one to cease protecting the Self from others but to welcome them into this one's mind, into this one's heart." (5-17-90-7-LJF)*

Karma will continue to exist as long as this man holds to the idea that others will take from him, as long as his intention is to protect rather than seek earnestly those who will receive what he has to give. Those not wishing to receive do not invalidate what he offers. Believing in his dreams and finding those who will receive will be this individual's first step in relieving his karma.

A reaction or non-productive attitude has its source in the inner Self needing to understand a particular quality or a truth. It is the way of thinking that is repeated from lifetime to lifetime until it is changed that produces the karma. When the attitude is changed it indicates the individual has matured to a new level of understanding. When one woman asked about her abandonment by her family during this lifetime and how it related to the past, the Reader responded:

> *"These are attitudes that this one has created concerning this one's own worth in relationship to other individuals. Would suggest to this one it is not situations and circumstances in the past that have caused the present attitudes; it is this one's desire for understanding that produced this one's creating the attitudes that this one does hold." (1-16-91-12-LJF)*

There have been readings done when the most significant lifetime was of a well-known and historically recorded individual. Even in these readings there is karma to be brought into balance. A female in New Orleans received a reading when she had been a famous musician in Europe, however, the name of the musician was not forthcoming. Perhaps knowing the name would have distracted this person from the present-day learning available. Another woman in Columbia, Missouri received a Past Life Reading when she had been the famed explorer Marco Polo. Throughout the present lifetime she had travelled extensively throughout the world, much like Marco Polo had done in his day. The significance for her was to follow through on what she had started and complete the things left undone in her life. In another instance a male in Norman, Oklahoma had been an English philosopher, Thomas Reid, in a past life. This lifetime was recent enough that he could find a listing in the encyclopedia. As he researched this historical figure, he was amazed by the corresponding information in the reading and in written history.

Déjà Vu

As I continued building mental discipline in metaphysics classes, the idea of karma and reincarnation from the standpoint of soul growth made more and more sense to me. It made sense that we would have more than one lifetime to complete all the learning and realize the potential of the Whole Self. It also made sense that each type of physical condition in life, whether living affluently or in poverty, in a healthy body or a disabled one and so on, would offer some type of learning for the soul.

I also began to get answers to some of the questions I had asked myself concerning my harp. It made sense that a fascination or familiarity with a particular time period or country was a good indication there had been a lifetime there.

One of my students received a Past Life Reading when he had been a Greek warrior. Even though he had not fully accepted reincarnation, he had always held a fascination with Greece especially of the time period of his reading. This fascination was the beginning of the verification of reincarnation for him in his own mind. A special talent or knack, like a craft or an art, is an indication that it has been done before in another lifetime and a certain amount of proficiency been developed. An artist in the present time learned from a Past Life Reading she had a great skill in creating art and different kinds of pottery in India in the 1700's. A student going to chiropractic school learned she had been a healer in China in the 1200's.

Also in developing my intuition and associating with those of like minds in the School of Metaphysics, my peers and I would often have "glimpses" of past lives. When I was playing my harp, one of my friends had a past life memory of my playing my harp in Greece. I had remembered a past life in early Greece when I had been a courtesan and had entertained many people with my music and dance.

Another friend related a past life memory of our being in a temple in Egypt. I asked her about it because I also had a memory of a past life when I lived at the Temple Beautiful and worked with musical tones and their effects on people and objects. She described a large, white, airy room, partitioned and decorated with soft gauze-like cloth that rippled and swayed in the wind of the open air. The gauze-like partitions diffused the sunlight outside. What she described fit the memory I had of the temple exactly! Music and dance were a large part of my study and research at the temple. The music I produced at that time had a haunting, otherworldly quality, much like the quality of music I now produced with my harp.

Another one of my classmates received a Past Life Reading

when she had been a Canadian Indian in northwestern Ontario in the eleventh century. Years before she had joined the classes, she had actually left her comfortable suburban life as a housewife and moved to northwestern Ontario to homestead. She lived out in the wilderness fifty miles from the nearest town and sixteen miles from the nearest road. She had no electricity, no running water, no flush toilets, no radio or T.V. But as rugged as her existence was she adapted easily, even feeling comfortable and at home. She didn't know why she felt so comfortable until years later when she received the Past Life Reading.

Each of us is unique. The identity we have built through the understandings gained is our process of discovering who we are as mental creators. We have proceeded according to our own choices. The soul has chosen to incarn into a certain physical condition in order to add an understanding to the Whole Self. The soul uses race, sex, nationality, physical features, parents and country as a means of stimulating this kind of learning. Being born into a pleasant situation is no more a reward than being born into an unpleasant situation a punishment for something done in the past. Both are offerings of something to learn. In fact, the learning from a challenging situation is often apparent because of the qualities utilized to respond with a sense of dignity. In either case it is how you use the life's situations that cause the growth.

What could be learned by being born into a wealthy family or a poor family? In one situation a female was born into a wealthy family in China to offer her a place to progress spiritually.

> *"We see this one actually believed that this one's own self-sacrifice and this one's own self-discipline would benefit and cause those around the self to evolve. We see that this one actually believed that in this one's own self-discipline, it would cause the commoners around the Self to evolve. And this was done for them, rather than for this one's own self-gratification. We see that the understandings built in that lifetime were primarily of self-control, self-discipline, of maintaining a sense of peace and calm, and of identifying this one's own source of being." (6-16-90-4-CSR)*

By the same token, a male was born into a family of nobility in France and dealt with a sense of value within himself. He ran away from the opportunity to use his situation and learn about value and thus did not add any growth to his soul.

> *"We see this one to be raised with the idea that this one was eventually to take over the position that this one's father had and we see this to be a position with the government. We see this one personally to think that this one was not capable of living up to the grandness and the reputation and the kind of honor that this one's family had. We see for this one to spend a period of time in hiding where this one did travel and did hide this one's identity and did pretend to be a peasant where this one did not have to live up to the types of expectations that this one had had." (7-25-90-10-LJF)*

Upon entering a new physical lifetime, the soul can choose the physical form that will accelerate learning. For instance, the soul will choose to be born into a male body for the opportunity to learn how to be aggressive. Being born into a female body gives the soul the opportunity to learn how to be receptive.

> *"We see this one to be utilizing the male form at that time to cultivate a certain type of aggressive expression. We see this one to be very conscious of this desire to do so." (6-22-79-1-SMB)*

A young woman asked why she had chosen to incarn in a female body this lifetime. The answer was very enlightening to her:

> *"There is a desire on this one's part to understand the process of creation. We do see that this one has practiced initiating action but that in regards to the commitment of the completing and receiving what has been initiated that there is learning that this one desires. It would be in regards to this quality of understanding that this one made this choice." (1-16-91-9-LJF)*

Being born into a particular country or a particular race affords the soul unique conditions in which to respond. One individual asked why he had been born in Iran. The answer revealed a particular quality that this country offered him, one that would stimulate him to bring out understandings of a poetic nature in the early part of his life.

> *"We see for this to primarily revolve around a love of beauty and the recognition of the beauty in thought and the recognition of the beauty in poetry, the recognition of poetry in life and the ability to view life as a poem or as a rhythmic movement. We see that this type of beauty is recognized only when there is the disciplining of attention and the disciplining of the ability to visualize not only outer things but inner things and how the inner things connect through their outer manifestations providing a link between the inner rhythm of what produces life and outer movement." (6-16-90-7-CSR)*

A female asked why she had been born in England in this lifetime and why she had been adopted. The answer included the need for particular astrological influences as well as early cultural training for her learning. The reading went on to say the birth condition did not matter, the parentage did not matter, as long as she had the conditions for building independence and self-reliance. This is an example of how the soul will choose the best conditions to learn the lessons that are most important. In this case the physical parents were immaterial as long as the opportunity for learning existed.

Another female asked why she had chosen to be born in the United States this lifetime. The Reader related that this country offered freedoms and therefore the opportunity for her to choose. The soul in choosing certain physical situations sets up a mental condition for learning. The soul makes these choices in regards to the growth of the Self.

In a past lifetime in France, I was born into a body that was deformed. A portion of the right arm was missing and the pelvic area had not been developed, making it difficult to stand erect or walk. My soul chose to be born into this physical condition for a particular reason. I asked about this reason in my reading. The reply was:

> *"....to consider that to deal with and confront the situations that occurred as a result of this selection was a great*

opportunity to find strength within the Self."   (10-78-1-
GAD)

When the soul chooses a difficult situation for the physical being, it offers an opportunity to build such qualities as strength or courage within the Self. How else will the individual know these qualities unless he faces a situation where he can exhibit and use them?

Possibility Thinking

This Past Life Reading offered a universe, as it seemed, of facets about myself – areas to build, develop and cause to mature.   In that particular past life, my family learned to accept my deformity but the community didn't. Early in life I had developed an image of myself as deficient and ugly. I also had great intuitive abilities and often had visions adding to the isolation and fear of myself and my family from the community.

My religious devotion was important to me. I would sometimes envision spirits of a religious nature that were highly revered. On two occasions during mass the congregation witnessed the presence of a light around me. Because the community was superstitious they reacted to me as a combination of demon and saint. It was not until the priests in the church announced that this translucence was from a spiritual source that I became accepted by the community. I even experienced some notoriety at this time as people desired counseling. During that time I took my attention away from my inner development and onto the popularity I was experiencing. I depended heavily upon attention and approval from outside influences for my sense of individuality and security. So much so that when the attention from the community had receded I experienced a sense of instability and confusion. I died shortly thereafter from a respiratory problem. The significance to that lifetime is as follows.

"We see in the present lifetime this one has carried through
and is dealing, in a conscious and unconscious fashion, with

> *many of the attitudes which were part of her innate self
> during that previous time period. We see this one to have the
> image within herself and to have had this since early child-
> hood of extreme plainness and unacceptability through her
> expression in the physical sense. We see this one has
> attempted and has utilized many ways to compensate for this
> feeling. We see this one so far has not successfully released
> herself from this visual image of herself. We see this one also
> to again have the tendency to place and identify the self
> through reactions and external situations. We see this one
> to depend to a great degree upon external situations as a
> measurement of her own place and her own individual self.
> We see this one to deal often with an inner sense of isolation
> which has no basis in fact, or is not produced in actuality by
> the situations and the conditions of the life. We see this one
> to suffer from this sense of isolation and to have difficulty
> breaking through the wall and the barrier which it presents
> to herself. Would suggest to this one to recognize that the
> conditions of the physical existence are those which have
> been brought to the self as aids and supplements, that these
> cannot and should not be relied solely upon as a measure-
> ment of success or existence. Would suggest to this one to
> recognize that there is and will continue to be an innate,
> sustaining movement of existence and progression which is
> not eliminated nor obliterated completely at any given time.
> Therefore this one need not be concerned to sustain that
> externally nor to create it or to initiate it for it is already
> initiated, but rather to observe it, to know it and to comple-
> ment it with that which is in the physical situation." (10-78-
> 1-GAD)*

It was as though the Reader had reached inside and touched the deepest
parts of my Self. She had touched the part of me that lives within four
glass walls and watches the world going by outside – the me that wishes
to reach through that wall and give, fulfilling the deep desire to share and
be a part of someone else's life. And in the giving I would not have to
fear rejection or loss.

    She had touched the part of me that tries to establish a sense of
Self according to what others think. In truth, I had ended up losing

myself in the process rather than building any image of my Self.

She had touched the part of me that reaches to be close to the creative, motivating force of the Universe, our Mental Father. The Reader had captured what could be within my Self with either its fullness and richness or its loneliness and emptiness.

There were so many parallels between that lifetime and this lifetime. I had experienced so often a sense of plainness and unacceptability. I had done many things to compensate for that feeling. As a child and a teenager I had strived to make good grades and be "the perfect girl" for my parents. I had made sure I was well-groomed and presentable to others. I had been active in my church and school through various clubs and organizations, scholastic and social. Yet inside I considered myself not good enough, always second best.

I had been afraid of being a bother to others so I would sacrifice my own need to avoid what I considered might take away from someone else's needs.

And then there was the strong parallel to know my God and to be close to my Maker. As a child I had wondered about the magnitude of God's love, if he cared about every hair on my head! During my life I had searched for the spiritual through my religious upbringing in my church, through the practice of Zen Buddhism in Japan and now through the study and discipline of the spirit in the School of Metaphysics. It had been a motivating force and focal point in my life.

From this reading I began to believe I was beautiful. Somewhere I had been missing that part by adopting an image of myself as plain and unacceptable. I didn't have to work so hard at being acceptable. I already was. All that was needed was to discover and embrace it.

I had begun to see how I could build an image of being beautiful and acceptable as a young adult. How I wanted to be beautiful! But I wasn't. I thought of women who had beautiful faces but were not beautiful. I thought of women who were considered plain looking but who radiated a beauty that went beyond the physical appearance.

"If this is so," I thought, "then that means if I cultivate the inner beauty I can actually become more beautiful the older I get!" I began to imagine what it would be like to bring out inner beauty. It was a delight to imagine that I could possibly cause myself to become beautiful.

This Past Life Reading was bringing out a possibility – the possibility of causing a change in my way of thinking that could bring about a change in my Self and my life. By getting a chance to look inside I felt closer to my Self and more integrated with the parts that were inside – the parts that were lonely and the parts that were beautiful.

By responding to the information and suggestions in the reading, I was removing misconceptions about my Self as unacceptable and isolated, learning that other people wanted to be close to me just as much as I wanted to be close to them. I made a point of speaking to people in my office or at the bus stop on my way to work as a way to reach out to them and discovered how easy it was to make friends. I was gradually recognizing my importance in the scheme of things and that I always had me to give in any situation. During an evaluation at my job, my boss commented on how much the morale in the office had improved since I had started working there and how I had taken a potentially strained situation between my Self and another employee and changed it for the better. I had a growing sense of contentment as I reached out to others. I was, in fact, causing my own evolution.

From lifetime to lifetime evolution occurs by fulfilling the desires of what we have to give and what we have to learn. When our choices benefit not only ourselves but others as well, then we are well on our way to progressing to the next stage of our spiritual development.

The Past Life Readings are an essential aid and basic prerequisite in the evolution of the spirit of Mankind toward understanding and fulfilling his highest potential. In order to do this, all must honestly face themselves, seeing real strengths and utilizing them to continually greater degrees as well as creating awareness and understandings in the blind spots of the Soul. All must release the inclination to hold back on their dreams. All must give, thus benefiting humanity while fulfilling the individual desires of the soul. Truly both go hand in hand, for in holding back what is being restricted is growth. Giving causes growth to the Whole Self. All must realize that they are not isolated islands but an important part of something greater than any one individually. And all must trust their inner knowing and give from that part of themselves. We are the ones. Let us move forward.

Born and raised in Oklahoma, Pamela [Carpenter] Blosser received a Bachelor of Arts degree from Texas Christian University with a double major in English and Sociology. In 1969, she embarked on a decade of world-wide travel including living in the Orient for seven of those years. While in Japan, Dr. Pam practiced Zen Buddhism and broadened her studies including skill in the Koto, the Japanese harp. In the late 70's she lived in London where she pursued Montessori certification. Upon returning to the States a year later, Dr. Pam knew she wanted to continue her spiritual studies and began classes in the School of Metaphysics. Since that time she has traveled the Midwest, living in seven major cities where she has taught hundreds of people the course of study offered through the School of Metaphysics.

Now based at the School of Metaphysics Headquarters on the campus of the College of Metaphysics, Dr. Pam serves in many capacities including: instructor in metaphysics and the fine arts, mentor for Spiritual Initiation Sessions, art & production manager for SOM Publishing, and director of the summer college preparatory camp for young people. After earning a Doctorate of Divinity degree in 1994, Dr. Pam became chaplain for the College of Metaphysics. She serves on the Ordination Board of the Interfaith Church of Metaphysics. By 1995 Dr. Pam culminated her formal metaphysical education by receiving a Doctorate in Metaphysics. She is currently writing a book on the topic of Self motivation. Dr. Pam and her husband Paul, a member of the headquarters staff, serve as proprietors for the Dream Valley Bed & Breakfast, a guesthouse adjacent to the campus.

"Since 1978, when I had my first reading, it has never ceased to astound me at the accuracy of your readings.....I have had eight readings done since 1978. When I have something I can't find the answers to, I request a reading. Because of my skepticism, I give no clues to the School - yet, these readings have been so accurate, I've finally come to taking them at face value as a helpful teacher. Thank you very much." — Janet Walls, Canfield, Ohio

"I have found two brothers that were discovered through Past Life Crossings. It helped me to understand why I felt so close to these guys I barely knew."
— Ida Smith, Clinton, Mississippi

"I want to tell you how grateful I am to you for the readings you have done for me in the past year. I believe the School of Metaphysics provides one of the greatest services to others that I have ever found...I would like to share at least a few of the ways in which the readings have benefited my life and other's lives too....In the summer I had a crossing reading. I was torn between whether to continue in a relationship I had or to discontinue the relationship. My grief at losing the relationship was immense but if I chose the relationship, my career would suffer. The reading suggested I look at the desires I had formed aside from the relationship and then see if the relationship fit with those desires. This suggestion enabled me to see that my goals and desires did not fit with the relationship. I am a chemistry student and would have had to drop out of chemistry to continue the relationship. Instead, I applied for a "cooperative education" program (like an internship) in St. Louis. The competition for this opportunity to learn on the job in the chemistry lab is intense. Yet, the interview went well and I was offered the position which I accepted! This is just another way the School of Metaphysics has made a difference in my life. I now have professional experience (and) have been well rewarded financially for my efforts." — Margaret Kick, Springfield, Missouri

"I requested a family reading for myself, my husband, and our three sons. At the time, I felt we were functioning as five individuals, and not as a family unit. Each person was attempting to go his/her own way, and I couldn't seem to pull (us) together...After receiving the family reading I then had a clear picture of the problems and personality conflicts involved. I was able to comprehend what each one of us as an individual is working on in this present lifetime, and what we are dealing with as a family unit...I highly recommend a family reading (for it) provides the necessary information and insights to those seeking growth in the family structure." — Lorraine Cochran, Tulsa, Oklahoma

"Thank you for the information your organization has sent to me in the form of Family Readings. I have since February 1984 received my first immediate-family reading, my second family reading in October with other members, and another with my present husband's family in December 1991. The information we all obtained has been extremely enlightening... If I can ever be of service to your organization, or to any other person in question of the value of the readings I am happy to do so." — Terri Pope, Houston, Texas

"The opinions which we hold of one another
our relations with friends and kinsfolks,
are in no sense permanent, save in appearance,
but are as eternally fluid as the sea itself.
—*Marcel Proust (1913)*

Crossing of Paths Readings
by Paul Blosser, B. A.

Have We Met Before?

Bruce was my best friend in the seventh grade. I was a ninety-five pound weakling, Bruce was twenty pounds lighter. I approached Bruce in the hallway on the second day of school, just after we left algebra class.

"Hey, aren't you in my fourth hour history class?" I asked, attempting to strike up a conversation. From that moment on, we were friends. We ate gruel together in the school cafeteria. We shot spit wads during history class while the teacher's head was turned. We both detested gym class when we learned square dancing and had to touch girls (how gross!).

We read MAD Magazine from cover to cover and we doodled endlessly. Bruce could draw the greatest Rat Finks with their tongues hanging out and driving the weirdest cars. His *pièce-de-résistance* was Snoopy the flying ace piloting his bullet-ridden Sopwith Camel and cursing the Red Baron.

We liked the same kinds of books and swapped library books back and forth. We liked fiction stories about heroes like Captain Nemo, biographies of great men like Harry Houdini, Thomas Edison, and Old Hickory. We consumed stories of adventure and intrigue. In fact, we created a wonderful Walter Mitty intrigue of our own. In our fantasy, we were heroes. One night, while most of the United States slumbered, the Communists bombed us and thousands of troops parachuted in and took over. Only Bruce and I could save democracy and the United States! Given the reality of 1967 and the creative genius of two teenage boys, we began making concrete plans–just in case! Bruce had some pretty wicked ideas about his pellet gun that also shot darts. We'd also break into sporting goods stores and steal ammunition and rifles. We'd make Malatov cocktails (I had to ask Bruce what they were) and build our own bombs. We developed our own secret code and tested it passing notes in history class. We plotted the best places to attack the enemy and planned ways to trap them.

Bruce and I enjoyed each other's company. It seemed like we'd laugh forever when we were together. Our imaginations were stimulated endlessly, by each other, by the books we read and the movies we saw, by the jokes we told and by the "cracked" perspective we shared on life, junior high school, and girls.

Our friendship and shared experiences grew during that two year period, seeded from an instant mutual attraction. I felt comfortable with Bruce the first time I saw him, almost as if I knew we would be friends before I ever talked to him.

You've probably had similar experiences of meeting someone for the first time and becoming best friends right away, as if you'd known each other all your life, or perhaps lifetimes. You find out that you have many of the same interests, perhaps similar backgrounds and experiences, common likes and dislikes.

You can probably recall a relationship that started with the mutual attraction of love at first sight. Or perhaps you'd describe your relationship to a person of the same sex as "sisterly love" or "he's just like the brother I never had". Your attraction to an older man might be attributed to the qualities you see in your father or grandfather. If asked to describe these types of attractions you would probably use physical or emotional terms. Yet this is only two-dimensional, like trying to describe a kitchen table in two dimensions; the table is three feet wide and thirty-two inches high. You have no idea how long the table is and whether you can seat four at your dinner party or twenty-four.

Although we are physical and emotional beings, we are also mental or spiritual beings. Incorporating the mental and spiritual perspective to a relationship is the third dimension of the relationship, just like adding the third dimension to our kitchen table! It is this third dimension to our relationships that explains what this mutual, instant attraction is and how it works. This added dimension adds depth to the relationship.

If you consider the physical laws of nature, such as the law of gravity or the law of magnetic attraction, then you can begin to understand the universal or mental law of attraction. Each of the mental laws are explained by universal truths; "what goes up, must come down" explains the law of gravity. Our mental law of attraction could be explained as "like attracts like" or, more precisely, "you will attract to you the people, places, and things that will offer you the greatest learning opportunities."

Like the laws in nature, the mental laws are impartial. These laws are always at work, for anyone, anytime, anyplace. You can demonstrate and experience the law of gravity at any time by dropping a pencil or sitting under an apple tree like Sir Isaac Newton supposedly did. You can experience the mental law of attraction by going to a movie or the grocery store, wherever and whenever people gather with a common goal.

So this concept of Universal Law and Universal Truth doesn't seem so far-fetched. If I go to the movie theater, everyone there has a desire to see the same movie. It makes sense that the people in my life are part of my life for a reason, that there is some common mental ground far more important than watching a movie.

This mental "real" attraction that draws us together is what manifests as the physical attraction or the emotional attraction. Although there are only a finite number of ways for a relationship to exist in our physical world such as husband and wife or lovers, as best friends, as business partners, the mental dynamics and possibilities of any relationship are as unique as the individuals involved.

What about the saying that "opposites attract"? The mental law of attraction still works, but what might appear dissimilar from the outside is built around common learning opportunities. Two people in a relationship may have diverse interests and backgrounds. Together, these two "halves" make a whole. Each person brings unique qualities and interests to the relationship. Have you ever dated someone who expanded your interests beyond baseball to music, art to science? Your partner can stimulate you to gain new experiences. Two friends, John and Laurel, illustrate how opposites attract and complement each other. Laurel enjoys literature, writing, and art while John's interests lie in team sports and golf. In relating to each other, they use the diversity in interests to try new experiences while sharing common goals. This stimulation and sharing is at the heart of all productive relationships with others.

Spirals of Growth

While I was in college, I dated a woman who was several years younger than I. She had never been married. I had been divorced and was a single parent. We dated for three years and talked about marriage and about creating our own advertising and public relations firm.

This had been a case of instant attraction. She attended a college in Louisville and returned to visit a friend, my neighbor, during spring break one year. We became friends and when she moved back to Oklahoma for the summer, we began dating. In the fall, she transferred to the University of Oklahoma where I was enrolled, so we could be together. During the next three years we were virtually inseparable.

She was struggling to be independent. Although she wanted to live her own life, she depended on her parents to pay her college expenses. I was trying to figure out what I wanted to do with my life. I'd set a goal two years earlier to finish a military career but medical conditions changed those plans.

In many ways, each of us had our future tied up in our relationship. I was a means for her to rebel against her parents since they didn't exactly approve of me, and she was my hope of a future. We built a dependency on each other as to who we were and what we wanted. I came to know that my identity was built around our relationship.

After we broke up, I was severely depressed and angry, and I took my anger out on the people in my world. It took many months for me to reestablish my own Self image and begin to see that I could accomplish what I wanted to with my life.

Each of us dealt with the breakup of that relationship. We didn't have the benefit of knowing how we could have more fully used the relationship as individuals while it was in progress. I had yet to learn about the School of Metaphysics and the service of Past Life Crossings.

I hadn't been studying metaphysics long when I heard about the Past Life Readings and Past Life Crossings. From a purely scientific and physical standpoint the idea that I had lived before made sense, after all the body I was using consisted of a small universe of atomic particles, electrons, protons, and neutrons. I knew that from eighth grade science class. I was a bundle of electrical energy and would always be in some form or another so the idea that I had been a physical human being before was not far-fetched. I also knew that I had a soul, but I had no concept of how or if it fit into the idea of reincarnation.

In fact, I didn't have that much of an idea about what reincarnation was. I knew that people in India believed in reincarnation. They believed someone died and came back as a cow. That part didn't make sense to my Western mind! It seemed preposterous that once I had achieved the status of a human being I would want to go backwards, expressing in what I considered a lower life form.

I decided to satisfy my curiosity and after some discussion with my teacher and school director, I decided to have a Past Life Crossing with my daughter, Michelle. She was ten at that time and I was a single parent. The school director told me the reading would reveal a significant past association Michelle and I had shared. She said Michelle and I had probably been together many times, and the reading would relate an association most closely matching our current relationship. She said the reading would aid our relationship and help me be a better parent.

As the reading session began, I was intrigued, nervous, and skeptical. After all, I was new to this and I barely knew these people. In fact, I had never met the woman who was reading the mysterious Akashic Records. The Reader and Conductor sat next to each other in the living room. A small table with cassette tapes and two tape players sat in front of the Conductor. Several observers and the people having readings crowded into the living room area, sitting on sofas and straight-backed kitchen chairs. A lone chair sat empty in front of the Reader and Conductor for the person receiving the reading. The Conductor began preparing the Reader for the session.

Once the session began, the Conductor looked at me and said, "Paul Blosser". I got up and moved to the empty chair. I knew that no one would see my sweaty palms, but I was afraid they would see my hands shaking.

"You will search for the identity of the entity referred to as Paul Gerald Blosser," instructed the Conductor. "You will search for a significant crossing of paths with this one referred to as Paul Gerald Blosser and that one referred to as Michelle Laura Blosser, and relate that significant crossing."

The Reader related that Michelle and I had been husband and wife in Germany in the late 1600's. Through my family trade, I was very adept (and stubborn) at my work in the garment industry. Michelle was a seamstress although she loved to care for and heal animals.

Okay, I could see how part of this could be true. There were many similarities between the past and present though some of them were what I considered vague. Michelle had a dog named Fuzzy and she loved him, taking good care of him. I had learned as a child to sew. In fact, I had just given Michelle a quilt for Christmas that I had made. I liked German food and studied German in college, but I figured this was because my family had been stationed in Germany when my father was in the Air Force.

I could also see that Michelle and I occupied similar roles within our association. Michelle had particular duties in caring for our home such as folding the laundry, doing the dishes, and vacuuming. And I had my prescribed duties as the head of the household such as paying the bills, cooking, and yard work.

The Reader stated that in our past association I believed in order and structure in life, living by rules and standards about how, when, and why things should be done as they were supposed to be done. Michelle however brought constant, spontaneous changes to our lifestyle which were very upsetting to me. Although this caused resentment in me, Michelle felt torn between her duty to me and her duty to the people in the community.

Part of this made sense to me. As the parent, there were certain rules and regulations I insisted upon; bedtime was 10 p.m. on school nights, homework and chores needed to be completed before playing, and Michelle was to ask permission to go to someone's house or to shop with a friend and parent so I knew who she was with and where she could be found.

"We see upon the part of the female that this one had a very great love for the one of the male, but we see that at the same time, this one felt as though this one owed those ones that came to this one for service. We see that this one saw the self as being torn between the wants and the demands of the husband and the needs of others within the community. We see however this one gave very little attention to this one's own needs and how each could satisfy the needs on the part of the Self." (1-9-88-5-GBM)

The reading revealed that in her past life Michelle's perception was one of sacrificing what she wanted so she could meet the demands of the husband and the demands of the villagers. Her resentment and frustration concerning this continued throughout that lifetime. Communication was a primary issue to be resolved between us in the past.

"We see that these ones continued in primarily the same manner throughout that period of time. We see that there were ways where the one of the male was constantly wanting something from the female, that this one was constantly trying to achieve and yet there was very little communication to exactly what this was or how, in fact, each could contribute one to the other and to the association." (1-9-88-5-GBM)

I could understand that communication was an issue in that past life and I knew that we each needed to communicate better in our current relationship, but I thought the same thing could be true for everyone in every relationship. However, as the Reader related how the past association was significant to the current relationship, my skepticism and doubt were swept away.

"We see that at the present time there is some frustration that exists in the one of the male once again. We see that the male does not see what this one does have to offer the one of the female. We see that there are ways that this one is aware of certain changes as they are occurring, but we see that this one does not cause there to be a preparation in this one's thoughts and this one's actions to be able to use the changes

> *to this one's own benefit as well as to the benefit of the female." (1-9-88-5-GBM)*

As a single parent, I was insecure in raising Michelle. Although I was the oldest of six children and I'd had plenty of practice taking care of and being responsible for others, there was still a part of me that didn't know if I could handle being a parent. I also felt there were things that Michelle didn't need to know until it was time for me to tell her, feeling that I had to protect her from disappointment. Her hopes had crashed many times before when either a planned visit with her mother or other major events didn't work out.

One of the things that intrigued me about the significance of the reading was the description of the thoughts we each held and how they were often very similar. I have always been one to analyze a situation or experience, trying to figure out what happened, why it happened, and how I could improve or "fix it". A perfect example of this is my affinity with machines (probably from a past life). I have never been afraid to repair something that was broken, whether it was a car, a clothes dryer, or a computer. I had often been puzzled in my life because I expected that everyone thought the way I did. The insights from my reading helped me see that my tendency to analyze is an exceptional quality rather than a norm. I began to appreciate the way I think and recognized at the same time that Michelle thinks in a very similar manner. She wants to know how to figure things out for herself also.

> *"....in regards to communication, that there be the recognition that there are definite differences in ways of thinking and yet there are definite similarities. Would suggest to the one of the male to listen very closely to the one of the female both when there is direct communication and also when that one is in this one's presence. This one will be able to hear many of this one's own thoughts as they are expressed."*

As the Reader said there were different ways of thinking, I recalled an experience Michelle and I had just a few months earlier. She had put dirty dishes in the dishwasher after school one day. After I came home from work, I discovered that she had not loaded the dishwasher the way I taught her! She was wrong I thought. Although her approach was different, her method worked just fine. From this I could see the rigidity in my thinking that was being pointed out from this past association.

I also remembered several instances where I had a doubt or was puzzling over something in my mind and Michelle would ask or say essentially what I was thinking. It was like she was speaking my thoughts because my thoughts would be out in the open for me to view.

After the significance was related I was permitted to ask any questions. I wanted to know how Michelle and I could use the information in our current father-daughter relationship.

> *"We see that it would be beneficial to both to recognize each individual's personal responsibility to themselves and in regard to the use of the association. This would not be the responsibility that oftentimes these ones slip into, of thinking they need to control one another, but it would be that which would bring the attention to the conditions and circumstances that enable these ones to follow through on their thoughts, to be consistent in their thinking and their communication." (1-9-88-5-GBM)*

This also made a great deal of sense to me. I worked many hours, attended my classes at the School of Metaphysics one night a week and served on several committees in the community. I felt like there were times when Michelle did give up the things she wanted because I had a meeting or other engagement. I often felt guilty and wanted to make up what I believed to be lost time with her. She would make deals to go to the movies; spending the night at a friend's house or having a friend sleep over. Each of us in our own ways influenced and tried to control the other to get what we wanted rather than communicating our desires and goals openly and honestly.

Several years ago, an attractive woman entered my life. Again there was an immediate attraction on both our parts. We talked easily and comfortably about children since we were both single parents, about metaphysics and our personal goals. We began a good friendship, and we both knew as she returned to her home, that there was more to this relationship.

Our relationship sky-rocketed several months later as we wrote fast and furiously, establishing a long-distance relationship that existed primarily on the telephone and in the mail. It was a great opportunity for both of us to express our thoughts and emotions. This was a different relationship for me, with a great deal of emphasis on mental and physical communication with very little physical time and contact. We decided to explore our relationship further and requested a Past Life Crossing. Because we'd each had readings of this type with other people, we knew we would receive an honest and objective perspective on our relationship. We also knew that we would gain a greater understanding of how we could aid each other in fulfilling desires and accomplishing goals. We would have the information to add on to that important third dimension of our relationship and we'd know how we could make the most of our physical and mental time together. In short, we'd know collectively what cards were on the table and how to play them.

Our Past Life Crossing revealed a significant relationship in England in the 1400's. The past relationship was significant because it related a previous relationship with mental attitudes and karmic learning opportunities paralleling our current relationship.

> *"We see for the one of the female to have been the mother of the one of the male. We see the one of the female to have been very domineering and we see that this one was very persuasive of what this one wanted. We see that oftentimes this one would attempt to manipulate the one of the son to do the things that this one wanted, for we see that the one of the son was often very stubborn and was reluctant in conforming to the rules and regulations." (5-20-90-1-SMR)*

The physical structure of the past relationship differed greatly from our present relationship as friends and lovers, but the mental and emotional perspectives were very much the same. In some respects though, the mother/son relationship co-existed within our current relationship. She was a very strong-willed and single-minded woman, willing to sacrifice or go to great lengths to accomplish her goals and desires. I counted on her for support, somewhat financially but mostly emotionally, during that time. When we talked, usually once a week, the long distance call was charged to her phone bill. There were many times, as we communicated by letter or phone, that I sought her emotional support, particularly when I was feeling sorry for myself or feeling that I could not achieve what I desired.

An issue surfaced in this reading that had been apparent in an earlier crossing with my daughter and in other readings I had requested. It pointed out a karmic lesson that I was beginning to recognize and deal with. The issue or karmic lesson that keeps appearing in my readings is the power of my influence. With limitations in my understanding of relationships with others, I often find myself trying to control another's attitude or action giving little or no consideration for their choices or desires. My learning in those situations is to recognize when I am being controlled and how I control others. This helps me to understand what my limitation is and why it exists, giving me freedom to change and grow in caring for myself and others.

I have heard people remark as they listen to a reading, "Oh no, am I still manipulating people" or "am I still doubting myself" or whatever a specific karmic issue might be for them. There are major karmic lessons to learn each lifetime, just as there are certain astrological influences that reflect throughout your life. I can't expect to have a single relationship where I complete all my karma about recognizing manipulation, and then never deal with the issue again this lifetime.

Karma is a universal, mental law. It is a magnificent tool for our awareness and enlightenment. Karma offers repeated opportunities to learn and put into practical application what we gain from our experiences. The operative force behind karma is intention. If your intention is to escape duty by having someone else do your work, like Tom Sawyer did while white washing Aunt Polly's fence, then as far as you are concerned you have unjustly taken advantage of another. The manipulation people fear or find repulsive occurs when only your best interests or selfish interests are served rather than the interests of everyone involved.

However, when your intention includes concern for another, you can use your influence productively to aid someone else. For instance, if our hero Tom intended to teach each of his helpers how to be the best fence white washers in Hannibal, Missouri, then his purposes would be just and advantageous to all involved. When you have an idea of how each person can benefit from an experience your influence is elevated.

At this point in my life, I was struggling with some major decisions about my personal growth, and the outcome of those decisions would impact the rest of my life. I felt like, once again, I'd set some goals for myself that I couldn't achieve. I was feeling very frustrated, as much with myself as blaming the world around me. I felt like I needed a refuge, a place to run away in case everything didn't work out. I viewed the relationship as a port to weather my mental and emotional storm and a place where I could hide.

> *"We do see however that the one of the son did have an attachment to the one of the mother and he did feel that this one needed to be of service to the mother. We see that due to this type of obligation, the one of the son remained in the home for a long period of time. We see however, even though this one felt obligated, there were many areas where this one would become very frustrated and very angry within the self, for we see that this one felt that he was cheating the self due to the fact that this one was not able to pursue many of this one's own desires." (5-20-90-1-SMR)*

One of the goals we wanted to accomplish with our reading was to develop a closer relationship although we were physically separated by hundreds of miles. We wanted to determine how we could help each other fulfill individual and common goals. In response to this, the reading had this to offer:

> *"....would suggest to these two that the importance is to have open and honest communication, for we see that at the present time period there is still a great deal of manipulation that occurs between these two individuals. We see that much of the manipulation is when each one feels vulnerable and feels that each one needs someone. Would suggest to these two that it is important for them to build individual strength as well as strength together." (5-20-90-1-SMR)*

Since our long distance relationship had been built over the phone and by mail, we prided ourselves on our communication and the ability to express ourselves honestly to each other. However, the Reader's insistence on "open, and honest" communication did not come as a shock to either one of us. I could recall conversations when I was feeling vulnerable, lonely, or uncomfortable with myself, where I left those undesirable thoughts and perceptions of myself unspoken. I sought instead to find my self-value or self-esteem in someone else's eyes, because through my own eyes, I didn't possess those qualities.

The Reader went on to suggest how I could use what I had learned in the past association to build trust in myself, in my thoughts, and practice open and honest communication.

> *"...it would be of importance for this one to practice courage in this one's own self and for this one to be able to speak up and speak this one's thoughts as this one thinks them, for we see that very often this one's victimized identity is due to the fact that this one does not express what this one has to say."*
> *(5-20-90-1-SMR)*

Truly open and honest communication is one of the keys to building and using any relationship. The idea of expressing thoughts openly and honestly incorporates trust in yourself, in your thoughts and their reality, and trust in the relationship. To use my association most productively, meant that it would be most productive for me to admit when I was feeling victimized or sorry for myself. It would give me the opportunity first, to admit such thoughts exist in my mind, and second, to physically hear my thoughts. With this type of honesty in communication, the relationship would also provide a place for me to gain another person's objective perspective as they presented truth to me about my own thoughts.

It is often very easy to "buy into" someone's limitations or poor image of himself, feeling sorry for them and supporting them when they are down. However, this is not the most productive approach. You can give them an honest and objective perspective to help them identify their thoughts. If they receive your honest communication, they'll have information to help them recognize why they have those thoughts. You offer insight to help them change their thoughts and self image.

The Secret of Intimacy

Physical closeness is not a prerequisite for a successful relationship. I have had relationships where I've experienced physical and emotional intimacy, but the most satisfying relationships I've had involved mental intimacy. You can be mentally intimate with someone else only to the degree that you are mentally intimate with yourself.

As you begin to recognize and acknowledge your thoughts, your doubts, fears and limitations, then you can also begin to recognize the same in your partner. This degree of mental intimacy permits you to work together to identify your individual strengths and build on them.

A married couple that lived in separate states requested a Past Life Crossing. She was a television executive and he was a senator in the neighboring state. They had decided to maintain a commuter marriage for career reasons.

In their past association, each admired and was attracted to the other. He was a Greek governor and she was his children's teacher. In the past association cited, the pursuit of their individual goals kept them from assuming a traditional relationship, so she and the children were in a household separate from his own. The Reader went on to say this was a way that the male controlled the female.

The significance for the current association is the same: stubbornness and individuality causes each to try to control the other. Their mental attention has been on what is missing from the relationship rather than how each can gain from the structure they've chosen, and how the relationship can be built and grow. The unique situation they've created with their relationship offers each much freedom in pursuing their individual goals that a traditional marriage would not. It also affords them an opportunity to develop that mental intimacy and challenges them creatively to make their physical time together productive and fulfilling.

Weren't You in Egypt, Say 800 B.C.?

Star-crossed lovers may have the mistaken belief that they were great lovers in a past life; Romeo and Juliet, Samson and Delilah,

Cleopatra and Mark Antony. Such thinking leaves little room for all the ordinary couples in history, couples like Ezra Haddim Hezediah and his wife Esther around 800 B.C. in the area we know now as Palestine.

In their present incarnation Esther and Ezra are Laura and Calvin respectively. Both are students and teachers at Schools of Metaphysics. Their past life association revealed physical circumstances that were very similar to their current relationship. In both past and present associations, spiritual duty formed a significant role in the lifetime at that time and served as a strong foundation for the relationship. It was at least part of the mental attraction that drew the physical beings together.

> *"We see for these ones to have been a part of a group of people whose affiliation was religious in nature. We see for this to have been Hebrew. We see that the families were very close and that there were many opportunities these ones had to be in the same physical vicinity of one another.*
>
> *We see for the one of the male to have been trained to tend sheep and we see for this one to have considered this a type of sacred duty. We see there to have been religious significance to this and we see that this one felt honored to accomplish this in the ways directed or expected by those in positions of authority.*
>
> *We see for the one of the female to have prepared for caring for large groups of people. We see that this was primarily involving that of preparing food. We see that this one took this responsibility in a serious way. And we see that this one, although there was a desire to experiment, refrained from it because this one respected the traditions and the significance of the position this one was being trained for. We see that there was a kind of respect that these ones held in regards to their own chosen duties as well as in regards to their relationship to each other."*

In the present time, Calvin and Laura have expressed a commitment to pursue their spiritual growth while aiding others through teaching spiritual principles.

Like Laura and Calvin, each party in a relationship has expressed some degree of commitment to the relationship. The commitment is not always a spoken or written commitment, yet it exists and can take many different forms. For example, in your relationship with your employer, you have made a commitment to perform a certain type of work for a specific number of hours for financial gain, medical and vacation benefits and security. In a relationship with a sibling there may be a commitment to listen to the other's problems or concerns, share the care and responsibility of aging parents or trade babysitting services. In a love relationship there is probably a commitment to be the "one and only" or "significant other" in someone's life, "to honor, cherish, and obey in sickness and in health".

Much of this type of commitment may be expressed as contractual commitment. Some form of contract, whether written, spoken or unspoken, is the foundation for the commitment.

The most beneficial form of commitment in any relationship is the mental commitment first to your Self and your learning in the relationship, and second to the other person and their learning in the relationship. This is a very personal and intimate application of commitment. This is the type of commitment evident in Calvin's and Laura's relationship. Each desires to aid the other in becoming the very best they can be.

To begin that process in any relationship, it is important to recognize how the relationship currently exists. The significance of a Past Life Crossing pinpoints the relationship as it exists now:

"We see once again for there to be common interests between these two and we see that there is a respect that these ones hold, once again in regards to duty or position. We see that there is much that these ones are seeking in terms of what can be brought to the positions that these ones hold. We see in this way there is once again the accomplishment of the type of respect and the type of openness to experiencing in terms of how each can affect others. We see there is a kind of admiration these ones have for one another in regards to this." (9-9-90-2-BGO)

When you make a mental commitment to a relationship, you are making a commitment beyond the physical and emotional needs of the individuals to the souls who are involved in the association. The ideals or desires of the souls determine where the relationship can go. As you examine the relationship from the perspective of the soul and the learning that can occur, you can determine spiritual goals for the relationship that are in alignment with the individuals. You know where the relationship is and you begin to formulate where you individually and collectively want to go. The focus of a mental commitment to a relationship centers around personal growth and soul progression. You are investing your Self in aiding your mate to achieve their soul's desires or helping them fulfill their "mission" for this lifetime. What a marvelous gift to offer the other half in any relationship, a commitment that says, "I'm going to do whatever it takes to make the most of this relationship for my Self and for you!"

Give me a Sign!

It is exciting to imagine the possibilities of past lives you've lived and past associations you've had. Perhaps you and your father were fellow trappers exploring the Northwest Passage or discovering trade routes to the New World. Maybe you and your boyfriend were landowners in China during the Ming Dynasty or alchemists experimenting to turn lead into gold. What if you were a sheriff in the Old West and your sister was the schoolmarm or the local saloon girl?

There are physical and mental signs in any relationship to give you clues about your past associations. For instance, common interests about food, music, favorite times in history, similar tastes in books or clothes or movies can all be relevant to your past association. The best indication of the past associations is your own intuition, your "gut" feelings. A mental clue to the significance of your relationship is to determine recurrent problems or challenges. You may discover that you and the other person get frustrated because you don't feel like you communicate your ideas completely. You may determine you both repress your anger at the other or express your emotions too easily.

Laura and I requested a Past Life Crossing several months ago. We shared living quarters at a School of Metaphysics Center. Laura directed the Center and I was her teacher and supervisor. The reading would help us to live and work together more productively. It would also provide information to help me be a better teacher to Laura and aid me to know how to help her gain more control in the events and circumstances in her life as she learned how to direct the school.

The afternoon of the reading, we were voicing our thoughts about the upcoming reading. "What do you think we were?" Laura asked as we washed a few dishes. She was referring of course to the structure of our past relationship. "I think we were probably father and daughter," I suggested, very confident in the recognition of my thought. As we sat in front of the Reader and Conductor later that afternoon, we discovered Laura was my stepdaughter in Turkey in 400 A.D.

Neither one of us seem to have a particular affinity for Turkish food, at least not that we are aware of. There seems not to be a collective affinity to that particular time period, peasant garb or anything that one might associate with that lifetime. My intuition however was accurate. Since I first moved to Michigan, I felt Laura was like a daughter to me, that she had been placed in my charge for her growth and development.

You may be able to assess what a past relationship might have been or where or when, but only with objective analysis can you understand the desires of the souls involved in the relationship. The important part about the Past Life Crossings is the depth and insight they afford on using the relationship and developing it from the soul's perspective.

The purpose of the Past Life Crossings is to reveal to you a past association that is relevant, karmically speaking, to what is going on in your life and your relationship at the time of the reading. It offers significant insight and information so you can be a happier, healthier, and more productive person by applying the reading to your life and relationship.

The Reader identifies your vibration through your name when the Conductor says "You will search for the identity of the entity referred to as John David Doe". This identification would be analogous to having a negative of a photograph, your vibration, and searching through boxes of pictures, the Akashic Record, for a picture that most closely matches that negative. When the Reader responds, "We have this", the picture of John David Doe that matches the negative has been found.

As the Conductor continues, "You will search for a significant crossing of paths with this one referred to as John David Doe and that one referred to as Jane Ellen Doe, and relate a significant crossing," the Reader's inner attention is directed toward using the vibration or mental negative of Jane Ellen Doe to find an Akashic picture of John and Jane together.

There may be many of these group Akashic pictures. Some of the pictures may match the negatives of Jane and John as they exist today, some may not. School of Metaphysics readings are designed to locate the picture or past association that most closely matches the current relationship. There may be pictures of John and Jane together in the Akashic Records but none of them match the negatives. This may be because the relationship is very distant or uninvolved.

Such was the case with Mary and her four-year-old daughter Aimee. Mary was divorced and she had agreed Aimee's father would have custody. Since Mary was following her own spiritual path, she knew it would be important for her to meet the spiritual needs of her daughter as well as her physical and emotional needs. The Conductor asked the Reader to find a significant crossing for the two. After a brief pause, the Reader replied, "This is not seen."

No past relationship was found which significantly matched the current relationship. This may have been because of Aimee's young age, a transitional period in the development of the relationship, or the fact that the two souls had not previously incarned together. The Conductor knew from his own past experience the bearing and value this can have upon a current relationship. He knew information could be gained about the present association which would be timely, accurate, honest and objective. He asked, "Are there any suggestions for these two entities in the present time period?"

> *"We see that in the present period of time these two have desires which are very similar. We see there are many ways in which these ones are alike and that the past understood experiences are similar. It is important for these ones to realize it is their own separate individualities that are stimulating in their friendship. We see that these two do want approval from each other and in some ways try to be too much like each other. It is important for each one to*

> *maintain their own sense of individual identity....in order for
> both of them to recognize their own true value as individuals
> and also for them to understand just because something is
> appreciated there is not a need to change to be like what is
> appreciated. That is a decision which needs to be made
> separately, separate from the appreciation."*

This portion of the reading points out how the relationship is developing and how Aimee as a child is developing. Mary is her role model and Aimee wants to grow up to be like her mother, her physical parent. This also conveys how Aimee is adopting and assuming her mother's attitudes of wanting to please and be accepted. With this knowledge, this issue can be faced and changed, particularly on the part of Mary, so each can evolve. This will change the course of their interaction in years to come rather than remain an issue they will confront time and again through the years.

Although it does not occur often, the lack of a significant past life association between two people does give them a great deal of freedom in how they create their present relationship. When no crossing has occurred, there are no karmic issues between the two people involved. This means they are free to create the kind of relationship they desire now. When this occurs, the assessment of the current relationship becomes even more important and meaningful for the two people involved.

Sometimes no significant crossing is seen, and this will occur because there are changes taking place individually or collectively in the present relationship. It has occurred several times when one person has been questioning the desire or need for the relationship to exist. Doubt and indecision will limit access to past life information because the "negative" is blurred and out of focus so no matching picture is found in the Akashic Record. When this occurs, the objective counsel given for the present time period can aid the individuals to move beyond the stagnation or confusion in their present association. Once these issues are resolved, past lifetime associations may become available for consideration.

Mary and Aimee's crossing offered significant insight into their relationship today which can aid them throughout their life as mother and daughter. Their reading illustrates the power and influence our thoughts have on our Selves and on the people in our world, how your thoughts and attitudes as a parent are reflected in your children from birth. The time from birth to seven years of age is extremely important for the physical and mental development of a child. When a baby is born, its conscious mind is like a blank chalkboard, clean and ready to be written upon. The conscious mind is that part of mind connecting with the physical organ called the brain. It is also the part of mind that reaches for experience.

During these first years our conscious perceptions, opinions, attitudes and prejudices are formulated based on our early experiences, relationships and the thoughts and attitudes of the important people in our lives. As children, we begin imitating our parents in action, in thought, attitude, and in Self image (see Health Analysis section).

Mary had been studying and applying metaphysics in her daily life, so she knew the importance of causing her thoughts and attitudes to be productive and positive. She asked what attitudes she could develop that would benefit Aimee.

> *"Would suggest to the parent that by setting an example by following through with what is started is the most important. It is also important for the child to see the parent fulfilling her own desires. We see that by any part of this one's life, living it to its fullest and living its principles would be being an example to the child. We see that besides the discipline and the follow through, there are not any other specifics in terms of how this one should train the child."*

As a single parent, I recognize thoughts I've had that I needed to give up some of my goals so I could be a better parent or so my daughter could have what she wanted. I think this is probably a universal way of thinking that we have to give up what we want, to sacrifice our desires in life to settle down and raise a family. This is an attitude of "this is what I want, but I know I can't have it".

Oftentimes this approach to life is accompanied by frustration, unhappiness, or "waiting until the kids leave home" to accomplish what you've felt like you've put off. In this instance, the Reader is telling Mary it is important for Aimee to recognize that goals are important and you can accomplish what you desire. The way for Aimee to experience that kind of success in her own life is for Mary to live that kind of success.

Mary is a nurse, working evenings. There is also the physical circumstance of living in a nearby but separate city. She was concerned about her physical absence from Aimee and sought guidance concerning this.

> *"We see that by establishing a way of study for the child, and also for the communication between the parent and the child as to the purpose of the parent's absence and also the communication of the love and concern towards the child, would establish the conditions that would need to be present."*
> *(12-6-88-6-CSR)*

The study that the reading spoke of was for Mary to develop a form of mental discipline that Aimee could use. The benefit for Aimee, even at her early age, would be increased ability to concentrate, a greater sense of Self worth and a more clear image of herself as "Aimee" rather than "Mary's daughter".

Communication once again is an important factor in this association. Children often blame themselves because Mommy and Daddy are divorced. They think they have erred, been a bad girl or bad boy, and feel physically and emotionally torn between the parents. This is usually the result of parental attitudes, training, and experiences projected to the child. The child reacts to the expectations of the parent. This reading stresses how communication can overcome a child's misconceptions and the resulting poor Self image.

It is important that Mary communicate the physical, emotional, and mental love she has for Aimee, demonstrating that love and concern for her when they are together. By expressing her desire to fulfill personal goals, Mary will aid herself and Aimee. Aimee will begin to formulate ideas of Self worth, accomplishment, and determination that will last her many lifetimes because Mary has given her an example to live by.

Karma: Haven't We Done This Before?

Has there ever been someone in your life who you reacted strongly to, that you couldn't stand? That reaction is a response to something that the other person represents within yourself and it may seem magnified many times. The people we bring into our lives offer us a place to reflect on ourselves, who we are and what we want to accomplish. Our outer world and its relationships are a mirror of our inner world and our relationships with ourselves. There is no such thing as a karmic boo-boo or a cosmic error. That person you're reacting to has come into your life for some reason. The two of you are together, no matter how brief the time, for your mutual experiencing.

One of my first teachers of metaphysics related the story of how her relationship with her boyfriend began. After she first heard of the School of Metaphysics, she received a call from Dermot, one of the instructors at the school, about a new class starting. When they first met, Denise knew they weren't going to get along. She described Dermot as pushy, aggressive, and a know-it-all. Denise and Dermot were very much alike. The words she used to describe Dermot also described her; she was persistent about achieving her material goals and pursued them with conviction and passion.

Dermot was a good teacher, stimulating Denise to examine herself and her thoughts. Her response was to become angry and storm out of the school after class. After some time, they requested a Past Life Crossing discovering they had been together in Germany and that Dermot had been Denise's older brother. He had teased her unmercifully and she would become angry refusing to communicate.

In a later Past Life Crossing, these two were engaged to be wed through parental arrangement. When they met for the first time however they set a mutual goal to not marry the other. They built communication, cooperation, and trust as their friendship developed and they accomplished their goal! During the months and years that followed Denise and Dermot eventually became classmates and peers. Their disharmony with each other changed to an attraction and they eventually became romantically involved. As their physical relationship evolved, their Past Life Crossings reflected a parallel evolution.

The Past Life Crossing offers suggestions about how you and

the other person in a relationship can use the learning from the past in your current association. The Reader and Conductor can provide an objective third-person view of your relationship so, if you listen to the information provided and apply it in your relationship, everyone concerned will benefit. If you apply the information today, the relationship will improve tomorrow.

The Reader and Conductor teams are trained to work together. They have studied the mind and its mechanics in great depth. They have applied mental law and mental techniques of discipline on a daily basis for years. Both the Reader and Conductor are insightful and also psychic. However, the information provided by way of the readings will not relate the future of the association.

A young student and her boyfriend requested a Past Life Crossing. They were at a crossroads in their association and wanted to gain more information, and to determine if they should continue the relationship. After the significance of the reading was related, they asked what direction they should take with the relationship. The Reader suggested it was up to these two individuals to determine what they wanted to achieve individually and collectively.

When we are born, we are endowed with two gifts, our own individuality and free will. Free will is our ability to make choices and we make thousands of choices each day. We choose our thoughts and words we speak. We choose what dress to wear, whether to fix meat loaf or chicken for dinner, what route to drive to work. It may seem that some of the day-to-day decisions you make are miniscule in proportion to the decisions that relate to soul progression and growth. As thinking men and women, with the ability to analyze and reason, we can choose our learning situations and what we desire to learn. The decisions you make today will affect your tomorrow.

In any association, you can choose what your purpose or mutual learning is and choose the future for your relationship based on how you and the other person in the relationship can use the relationship productively.

When requesting a Past Life Crossing, it is a matter of courtesy and respect for the other party to ask their permission to obtain the reading. After obtaining a friend's permission for a reading, a woman was concerned because the friend did not believe in reincarnation. She thought perhaps her friend's denial would somehow affect the outcome of the reading. The Conductor assured her that the information presented would be unaffected and accurate. Just because someone doesn't know where the library is located, doesn't change the information stored in the books at the library.

A woman called to ask questions about the Past Life Crossings when I was directing the School of Metaphysics in Norman. She had heard about the readings from a friend and wanted to get a crossing with her mother. During the process of the conversation I found that the woman's mother had passed away several years earlier. As we continued the conversation I informed her that a past life relationship could possibly be found, however there would be no relevance to her current relationship since her mother was deceased. Her curiosity would have been satisfied as to who they were in a past association, where they were and what they were doing, but there would be no useful information that she could apply in her life. In short, it might have made interesting conversation at a party, but provided no real service to the woman.

We recently received a very touching letter from a man in Caracus, Venezuela requesting more information about the Past Life Crossings. His wife had picked up a brochure about the readings several years earlier when they lived in Boulder, Colorado where he was attending college. At the time, he didn't pursue his wife's interest or desire for a crossing. He wrote to say their relationship had changed. He and his wife were experiencing difficulties. "We seek your help. We are lost. Help us find our way."

Change in life, in any form, can be frightening and threatening. Oftentimes we'll do anything to maintain the status quo, but when the situation is forced we'll do something about it. We think nothing of changing the oil in a car every 3,000 miles or tuning the engine or rotating the tires so the car will continue to function. That's called proper maintenance. When it comes to other, much more significant parts of our lives, we'll bargain, ignore, and become angry to maintain a sense of balance with very little thought of "proper maintenance".

A Past Life Crossing is an excellent tool to aid the longevity of your relationship, like your car it is a vehicle requiring maintenance and diagnosis. Your relationships are vehicles for your soul growth and evolution as well as your partner's.

The Past Life Crossings are a service that is provided to the communities where Schools of Metaphysics are located and to cities where trained Reader-Conductor teams schedule visits. The information presented in the readings is to help you and those others in your life to live happier, healthier, and more productive lives. We all want to know that we've made our mark on the world, left something of importance behind, touched a few lives and made a difference in the world. The information is presented to you openly, honestly, and objectively with the best wishes for its use, and your growth and soul evolution.

Paul Blosser has been teaching applied metaphysics since 1987. He has lectured to business and professional groups, church and single groups, about dreams, time management, goal setting, creating happiness and wealth, stress alleviation and job happiness. Having completed an intensive eighteen month course of study at the College of Metaphysics in Missouri, Paul now travels extensively with his own computer consulting firm. When not on the road, he lives (and his wife Pam) on the campus of the College of Metaphysics. Paul holds a B.A. in Journalism from the University of Oklahoma and is currently pursuing his doctorate in Applied Metaphysics through the School of Metaphysics.

"The family is the association
established by nature for the supply
of man's everyday wants."
—*Aristotle (4th c B.C.)*

Family Readings
by Daniel R. Condron, M.S., D.M.

Choices of the Soul

Have you ever asked yourself, "Why was I born in this family, with these parents and older brothers or sisters?" Have you ever wondered, why did *I choose* this family to be born into or why did I *choose* my mother and father for this lifetime?

"But," you exclaim, "I did not choose my parents. I didn't choose the time period, day, month, and year I was born. Nor did I choose my place of birth. Neither did I choose whether I would be male or female this lifetime!"

Oh, yes, a part of you did choose. Each individual is endowed with free will and has this free will whether in the physical level of consciousness or not, whether before or after a lifetime.

I was born into a family with two older siblings. In addition to these two older sisters, I have a younger brother and a younger sister. For many years I questioned why I was born into this situation. Why did I choose a farm family in which there were many aunts and uncles, grandparents and cousins from both sides of the family living in close proximity? Why did I choose to be born the same year that the double helix structure of DNA was discovered? Why did I choose to be born in 1953, a year in which there was a conjunction of Saturn and Neptune which only occurs every 144 years? These are the kinds of questions that deserve an answer and I believe everyone has the right to have the answers to these and other questions about themselves, their choices and the meaning of life.

The Family Reading developed by the School of Metaphysics provides insights into many questions the individual may have about Self, his upbringing, relationships with family in the present and the source of many present day difficulties and affinities. Did you ever ask your Self, why did dad always seem to like my brother more than me or why was mother always so strict with me but not with my sister? Or perhaps your father or mother seemed to favor you over your brothers or sisters. By investigating a past lifetime in which the family members were together, the origin of present day relationships and attitudes within the family can become more understandable.

The nature of past life associations and their impact on present experiences is increased when you can accept that you exist beyond your physical body. The physical body is a vehicle that you, the soul or spirit, use each lifetime. Between lifetimes, you exist in the soul body or vehicle of the subconscious mind existence while assimilating the previous life's experiences and preparing for the next lifetime. Therefore, each lifetime is to be used to build greater wisdom, learning and understanding within the individual. After many lifetimes of learning the Self achieves full enlightenment sometimes referred to as the Christhood. Having learned all the lessons the physical has to offer the individual need not reincarn into the physical existence, but rather progresses on to a higher plane or level of existence.

Throughout your lifetimes you have been associated with many, many people. Many of these individuals you have had close associations with in the past, both pleasant and unpleasant. The choice to incarn into a specific family this lifetime, relates to the experiences the soul has had with members of this family in past lifetimes, although the exact relationship in the past may be different from the current familial relationship.

A Family Reading is a very special type of Past Life Reading for this reading presents to the current family a previous lifetime in which they were associated. The Family Reading can include up to five people in an immediate family. It investigates the association of these people in a significant past life time period. Through research we have found the probabilities of up to five individuals sharing the same previous lifetime experiences remain high. When more individuals are added the probabilities of common past life experience with all members diminishes considerably.

Many times people desire this information to improve their present family life. For example, a husband and wife who have three children may desire to understand this relationship better in order to be more effective parents. A Family Reading will provide these parents with valuable information about themselves and effective changes they can make for their own betterment and the improvement of the family life.

At times a family may request this type of reading and want to include a grandparent in the reading. This is possible as long as the number of people in the reading does not exceed five. The closer the kinship in the present, then the more likely a time period in the past when these five were together exists because of the group karma those individuals need to complete. The more distant the kinship in the present time, the less likely all five have been together in the same time period of a lifetime prior to the present one. Learning that was begun with these individuals in a past lifetime can be enhanced and added to in the present time period through association with these same entities.

In the present life we may have a father, a mother, a daughter, and two sons. In the past life, it may be that the present-day daughter was the past-life mother and one of the sons may have been the father while the present-day father and mother may have been the children in the past lifetime. Or the parents of this lifetime may have been grandparents of that past lifetime, or perhaps cousins. To someone not acquainted with the people receiving the reading, it can be confusing to follow the different relationships of the past. But to those involved, the previous relationships answer many questions and shed light on present-day harmonies and disharmonies. This is why we always provide an audio cassette of the Family Reading. By listening to the recording of the reading many times, much more of the information is assimilated and can be applied individually and collectively.

One Family Reading included Jason, the son; Joseph, the father; Ethlyn, the mother; and Melissa, the daughter. Their past life relationships proved to be very different from their present life:

"We see for these ones to be within the area referred to as China. We see for these ones to have come together when a marriage was arranged between the one referred to presently as Jason and the one presently referred to as Joseph. We see that the one referred to presently as William Joseph was in female form at that time. We see the female to have entered into the household of the husband, the one presently referred to as Jason, and we see for there to have been conflict immediately between the one presently referred to as William and the one presently referred to as Melissa. We see for the one presently referred to as Melissa to have been the sister of the one presently referred to as Jason. We see for these two women to have clashed and we see for them to have experienced jealousies and envies in their physical situation.

We see that the one presently referred to as Melissa did not believe that she would marry. We see that there had been several attempts to arrange this but there had been something that would occur, whether it would be the death of the intended spouse or some other offer that would be made to the intended spouse that would be better or would be taken, and this left her without a mate. We see that this had occurred several times, and that she had begun to believe that she would never marry. We see therefore that she did not want her siblings to marry either, particularly this brother because she was very attached to him and was very fond of him and did want to control his life.

We see that in many ways she did view the one presently referred to as Jason as a substitute for the husband she did not have. We see that there was not any overt physical affection between them or sexual involvement but we see that in her mind she did rely upon the one presently referred to as Jason for protection and for many of the securities that she would have expected from a husband. Therefore when the wife was brought into the household she very much resented this and we see that she did try to undermine the marriage. We see that the one presently referred to as William, the wife, was very meek and was introverted. Therefore it took her a while to realize the amount of animosity that was being directed toward her."

This reading continues describing the interaction between these three family members. The fourth family member, the present-day mother Ethlyn, enters the group association as the child of the couple described:

> *"We see that the child was female and that this again added another element to the dynamics of the relationship between all of these ones, for it was another female force which as she grew older learned the jealousies and the introversion of the two primary females in her life, and we see that in effect it was the female child who began to gain all the attention of the male." (10-6-92-1-BGC)*

The family dynamics of the past life, even though different from the present, still impact the familial relations of today. As the past life portion of the reading continues, the interactions between the four are described in detail and the significance to the present lifetime is related. In the present life the son and mother continue their tendency toward siding with one another as do the father and daughter, often facing reactions of jealousy once again.

In all Family Readings given, by using the names of people of the immediate family we have been able to locate a significant association in a past time period when all five were associated in some way. In fact, very rarely is the association of the five in the past life the exact same in regards to the blood relationship as it is in the present time period for the soul has many different lessons to learn in evolving toward enlightenment.

The Soul's Lineage

Each lifetime provides a different set of situations and circumstances, a different "classroom" in which to learn and grow. In school, you may take a course in chemistry, another in languages, and still another in history. Many different courses are required in order to learn the lessons necessary to graduate from high school and earn a diploma. Similarly, through many lifetimes the soul incarns into different environments, sometimes in a female body, other lifetimes in a male body. Between lifetimes the soul exists in subconscious mind for the subconscious mind is the abode of the soul. The soul will incarn in one race, and the next lifetime in a body of a different race. Each of us in our soul travels have incarned in many places on this earth, from Europe to Africa to Asia to North and South America.

Each individual has a unique purpose. It is the duty and responsibility of each individual within that family to discover their purpose for choosing that particular family in order that they may use the association to the fullest. Insight into these purposes is revealed in the significance of the past life association to the present life. This is illustrated from the reading cited earlier in this way:

> *"We see once again for the commonality between these ones to be in how they are motivated. We see that once again there is a need for external motivation for all of them to be able to move forward in their thinking. We see that they are often prone to falling into rash decisions or opinions which actually do not have much of a foundation, and we see that in doing so these ones rely upon each other for support of their opinions or belief.*
>
> *We see that many times, as was in the past, this is not in a productive sense to find courage in confidence in being able to reproduce but rather it is in being able to justify their limitations...*
>
> *We see that there is a great sense of connection that these ones have, there is a very real sense of bonding that these ones have, and we see that no matter what disagreements they may entertain or what kinds of conflicts arise, it does not hinder the bond. We see however that there is an attempt upon these ones part, once again, to expect a kind of magical revelation from the bond in producing understanding. As was in the past this did not occur, and it does not occur in the present.*
>
> *We see there is some need on each one of these one's parts*

to recognize that understanding is the result of individual desire and effort, it is not something that occurs merely because situations force the self into understanding. We see that each one of these ones are capable of much greater understanding than they give themselves credit for in the present time period..." (10-6-92-1-BGC)

This reading goes on to give suggestions for change to the family as a group as well as offering specific insights for each of the four family members. Jason is encouraged to face what is unpleasant rather than becoming distant and backing away when conflicts arise by creating a fuller realization of responsibility for Self and his life. William's tendency toward vacillating between stubbornness and indecisiveness is noted as a root for personal and family frustration. Suggestions for contemplation and reflection on ideals and purposes are given. Melissa is described as dynamic and aggressive, having powerful influence in the family. Her short-sightedness and narrowness of vision causes her to discount this, thus becoming irresponsible. She is encouraged to extend her thinking into the future to realize her influence over a prolonged period of time. Ethlyn's attachment to people causes her to change loyalties easily, leaving her dependent and needy. Ways of developing confidence in weak areas are outlined to aid in her individual growth and progression. When put into practice, the specific suggestions for the individual family members will improve not only their relationships with each other but with others in their lives.

Within an immediate family, there needs to be a variety of different associations so that individuals can experience different kinds of learning. The father in this lifetime may be practicing authority while the son is developing trust, follow through, and discipline. Some of the types of understanding or permanent learning that a person can develop in a lifetime are: discipline, pride, authority, love, value, respect, follow through, will power, receptivity, reasoning, intuition, determination, perception, communication, power, commitment, and Self motivation.

A Family Reading provides a case history of that particular family. The significant events of the past lifetime many times parallel events of the present association in the way that people act, react, and respond to each other's desires. You might consider this to be the soul's lineage, its roots so to speak. For just as an individual may investigate his family tree, discovering his physical ancestors, so he may also desire to know the history of his soul and the other souls he has associated with throughout history.

Our individual karmic obligations become apparent as we interact with others, and family units often reveal commonalities in the need for understanding certain qualities. These commonalities can be described as group karma. Group karma is often addressed in the section of the reading called the significance. This part of the reading shows how the past lifetime is relative to the present. One family discovered how to more effectively use their emotions in order to deepen communication:

> *"In regards to emotional issues that have already been described, there has been a tendency within this group for there to be a siding. We see that it comes in a variety of forms and combinations. There is no one that is more prominent than another and this was true within the past lifetime related as well. This tendency to look for support does cause there to be a division within this unit. It does cause there to be misperceptions and misconceptions upon each of the individual's parts. Would suggest that these ones cease to take hearsay about what another has said or done and begin to communicate more directly with one another. This would be of great benefit in causing there to be the unravelling of some of the emotional disruptions that occur in this group and it would aid these ones to be more open and honest with themselves in being willing to if necessary confront one another with ideas, opinions, issues, that have not been resolved. Would suggest to these ones there is no excuse for these not being resolved for we see each one of these ones to be intelligent and we do find for each one of these ones to have a concern and caring for one another. Would suggest that this be where the attention is focused and that the communication come from this place."* (5-25-91-3-BGO)

Another reading identified the need to learn to listen as the group karma experienced in the family. It aptly describes the individual karmic indentures, how they are similar in each family member and how they can use their relationships with each other to gain permanent understanding.

> *"We see that there is a need for all of these ones to build their listening capacity for we see that for the most part they all can be very vocal in expressing themselves, but we see that their listening capacity is not equal to their ability to express. It would be of benefit to all individually and collectively for the listening skills to be built for this would enrich their individual communication whether between one or two of them or all of them. It would also alleviate many temporary misunderstandings that do occur in their association.*
>
> *We see that there are many aspects to these associations in terms of how they impact one another; in terms of dependability, reliability, and dependence. These are basic issues that these ones are confronting within the associations. Would suggest that these ones keep these in mind when there are dealings (with each other) and attempt to remain as open and as honest about themselves as they can in regards to whether their sense of individuality is being lost because of dependency or if there needs to be listening or expression or if there is a tendency toward talking to one of the other people rather than talking directly to the person that they need to talk with."* (12-14-91-15-BGO)

Sometimes, the karmic similarities are less pronounced particularly when one or two members of the present family were more distant relatives or merely family acquaintances in the past. In one reading, we find one member of the present family was not a member of the family in the past lifetime related. This individual was, however, associated with the others. Two of these attended school together in their later school years, and they established a friendship based upon their academic interest. In later years they worked together to bring about academic reforms developing scholarship programs as well as incorporating practical study in a program that previously had been mainly theoretical. Roles can change in various lifetimes, yet we have chosen to be with the people that are close to us today in order to continue the learning that may have begun many lifetimes ago.

In addition to information concerning the relationship of the five to each other, the Family Reading can provide information about the land area or country in which this association took place, the time period and the occupations of the family members. Consider these excerpts from a Family Reading dating back to 340 B.C. in Peru:

> *"We see for these ones to have been what is referred to as Inca (or pre-Inca). We see for the one presently referred to as Anna to have been the daughter of the one presently referred to as Charles. We see for the one presently referred to as Charles to have been in female form and we see for that one to have been partnered with the one presently referred to as Tonya, who was in male form. We see for their association to have been one of necessity. We see that the marriage had been arranged and had not been from choice and we see for the one presently referred to as Tonya to have resisted this. We see that there were very definite ideas that this one held of what this one wanted to accomplish and what this one wanted to do with the life and did not at the time of being married have anything to do with marriage. We see however for there to have been much pressure that was placed on that one to move in that direction and we see that because this one wanted to attain certain positions within this group of people this one did accept this...*
>
> *We see that the one of the child, the one presently referred to as Anna, did have much of the mother's attention and we see that the one of the husband paid very little attention to the child until she began to exhibit types of intuitive visions. We see that this did gain the attention of the father and we see that it was at that time that the one presently referred to as Debora did become involved more directly with this family unit.*
>
> *We see for the one presently referred to as Debora to have been in female form and to have been the daughter of what would be termed the shaman within this particular group of people. We see that because she was the daughter of that individual this one had much information and was privy to*

much knowledge in regard to the duties and functions and abilities of the shaman and we see that there was a closeness that developed between that one and the one presently referred to as Tonya, the husband....we see although there was a closeness between these two and a kind of friendship which was not commonplace in this group of people, it was very natural for the one presently referred to as Debora and there was no questioning it. ...

We see the one of the male did bring the daughter to the one presently referred to as Debora and this was for a kind of evaluation. We see that the intention upon the part of the father was to gain some training for his daughter from the shaman. We see that it was through a variety of what could be termed tests that the one of the daughter did prove herself and we see that this was when the one presently referred to as Debora did serve as a communicator to the shaman of this young girl's abilities. We see that many of her abilities were in regards to a kind of healing...." (5-25-91-3-BGO)

This reading continues to describe the past associations incorporating two more family members and revealing more information about the Inca way of life during that time period. At one point it states that these people were invested in the Inca way of life, holding a great respect for tradition and ancestry. The information given concerning the land area, people and their culture is fascinating, but the true value of the past revealed in Family Readings remains in the relationships of those involved. In each crossing, the major attitudes and activities of the family members are revealed and the historical accounts appear as they are relevant to those activities.

Common Dreams, Individual Learning

In each Family Reading the relationship and significance of the past life association to the present life family is given. This section of the reading, called the "significance to the present lifetime", offers a wealth of information about how to improve the relationship among the people requesting the reading. It also offers valuable insights into how each member of the family can improve themselves. Topics covered vary from communication to discipline, from pride to love, from concentration to Self value.

A variety of troubling attitudes can also be identified. Guilt, doubt, fear, condemnation, anger, hatred, resentment or need for purpose in the relationships will be described when appropriate to the individuals requesting a Family Reading. The present-day significance for the family previously associated in Peru began by identifying the ways of thinking they have in common. It continues on to describe how each family member relates to the others:

> *"We see within the present period, there are very definite attitudes that hold these ones together and that are shared. We see that these also cause the points of conflict. We see that each one of these ones are very unique individuals with varying degrees of strength in the personalities. We see that these are very similar to the past lifetime related.*
>
> *We see within the present the one of Tonya to be the strongest of the members within this family and we see that the one of Debora also displays very definite attitudes and very definite strengths. We see that the influence these ones do impact upon one another and upon the remaining family members cause a kind of influence and repercussion in terms of the way that they think and the way they communicate. Once again the initiator much of the time is the one presently referred to as Tonya and we see that there is a kind of responsibility this one does take for causing the climate of this family to be as it is. We see this one often feels responsible for the attitudes and moods of other people even though this one will not take action upon it, whereas the one presently referred to as Debora does take action upon it. We see once again for her to often be in a kind of counselor role. It is often this one who does hear the opinions, ideas, or difficulties of the ones of the others particularly the ones of Anna and Avram. We see that once again those two do look at life in very physical terms and we see they become very*

opinionated as a result of it. We see that there is a kind of limiting of vision that occurs within those two as well as the one presently referred to as Charles. We see the one of Charles however to become much more stubborn in this one's attitudes than the ones of the other two. We see therefore for there to be more communication between all of these ones except the one of Charles."

The reading continues to elaborate on the specific attitudes held by each family member: Charles' isolation and egotism, Debora's irritation and need for love, Tonya's frustration in trying to control the lives of the others, Anna's sense of failure, and Avram's selfishness. It offers suggestions for personal change to each family member, then gives the following suggestion to the family as a whole:

"We see once again there are psychic abilities, particularly upon the part of the one presently referred to as Debora, and we see that there is much that could be developed in this regard as well for we see all of these ones take for granted much of the communication that goes on between them which is telepathic in nature. Would suggest that these ones begin to examine this. We see that these ones impact one another very strongly emotionally and there are very strong emotional bonds between these ones. It would be of benefit for these ones to learn how to separate the emotions from their own patterns of thinking. We see that there are similarities in the ways these ones think but there are very individual ways also and for the health of each individual concerned it would be of benefit for these ones to independently examine this and to begin to separate their own thoughts and emotions from that of each other so there could be more insight and control of the selves and therefore more of a recognition of their own sense of identity." (5-25-91-3-BGO)

This family is a close-knit unit in the present lifetime, frequently interacting. The choice for consistent interaction affords them frequent opportunities for Self examination and growth through using the family ties. As time passes, some families drift apart. Separated by physical distance, opportunities for interaction decrease. The following reading addresses this, offering a way to strengthen familial relationships:

> *"We see within the present period of time that because of the goals of each, as well as the lack of attention, these five do not really come together. We see that it would benefit these ones to establish some kind of common goal and purpose for their relationships with each other to center around."*

The reading elaborated on this point later, when a family member asked for more information concerning the common dream these ones share.

> *"Each one secretly fantasizes about how people would relate with each other in an ideal way. Each one has an idea of what they think the ultimate achievement for an individual is in terms of what mankind is reaching for and as to what they as individuals are reaching for or to become. We see that each one also does have some images that they normally keep fairly secret from each other in terms of their beliefs about life, death, the purpose of life. Some of them share with other people slightly but for the most part, each one of these ones as individuals keep all of these ideas and things which comprise their dream of what they would like to be to themselves. Therefore there is not the ability to work together as a group to achieve it. We see that a few of them have found other individuals who think along some of the same lines that they share some with but there could be much more learning within the family as well as outside of the family if they would start speaking these things. Their dreams would also become more clear in their conscious mind and realization if they spoke out loud these things which they hold secret in regards to this dream now."* (1-9-87-1-CSR)

By using this part of the significance given in the reading, this family is more aware of the need to set family goals. In a productive association there need to be common goals. These goals give the members of the family a common direction in which to move the family. For example, growing up on a Midwestern farm provided me a family with a common goal of raising crops and livestock. I had regular chores about the farm such as feeding the hogs and cattle and milking the cows. In addition, during the summer I helped my father plant corn and soybeans. I and my brother also worked with our father to cut hay and put it in the barn for storing until the following winter. My mother and sisters sometimes aided with the equipment and livestock. They worked in the garden growing foods to be eaten or canned and stored for the winter. So you see, we worked together as a team towards the goal of producing food, shelter, and clothing for our family. This working together process created a closeness among all of us that continues to this day. There is the need to communicate the hopes, desires, and aspirations of one to the other so that family members are aware not only of the source of their differences but also of the common bonds that keep a family together.

Another Family Reading brings out the need for common learning in the family, explaining the relationship of individual growth to familial learning opportunities. The reading reveals the cause of family members feeling isolated or apart from each other. Until each family member recognizes his or her part, the family remains distant parts of a whole and cooperation is absent. The main focus in this reading is for the family to identify the learning that is available through this group both individually and as a whole. The qualities of cooperation and communication need to be developed here as well as common goals and purposes. By communicating, these individuals become a family in more than name only, working together to accomplish goals.

In some Family Readings the significance begins by presenting suggestions to one member rather than the group as a whole. The following reading identifies the key person in the family. In the present day Robert is Terri's husband, Virginia is Robert's mother, Carol his sister, and Beau is Terri's natural son who has been adopted by Robert.

"We see once again for these ones to impact one another in very definite and individual ways. We see that there is a kind of collective consciousness which revolves around the one referred to as Robert. We see that in many ways that one is the connecting link between all the others. We see that therefore there is much that can be learned in terms of the relative positions of the male and female in regards to their association.

We see once again there is a tendency upon the part of the one of Robert to be somewhat retired in this one's abilities to deal with emotional issues. We see once again there is awareness that these need to be responded to, and there is the willingness upon this one's part to make conditions as such that they can be dealt with. This one does tend to postpone his own development in that way. We see that this is encouraged by the ones of Virginia and Carol, this postponement, but the coming to terms with this is encouraged by the one of Terri. Therefore there is a kind of jealousy that occurs between the ones of Virginia and Carol toward the one of Terri. We see that there is some feeling upon the part of Virginia and Carol that they cannot offer the one of Robert what the one of Terri can. Would suggest to those ones in that regard that this is true and that it does not in any way reflect badly upon them. Nor does it cause there to be reason for dislike or discredit or devaluing of themselves or the one of Terri.

Would suggest however that these ones come to terms with this and recognize the value of what they as individuals have to offer. We see that this is still a significant difficulty upon the part of the ones of Virginia and Carol that they still have a tendency to devalue who they are as individuals and what they have to offer. This is much of what their learning is centered around in the present time period, once again. The one of Robert stimulates their individuality and therefore can assist them in developing this.

We see that there is also some assistance from the one referred to presently as Beau in terms of this one's ability to stimulate a kind of inner desire within all of these individuals toward that which is beyond the physical, toward that which could be termed spiritual, toward that which could be seen as new and inviting and exploratory." (12-14-91-14-BGO)

At the time of this reading Beau was just reaching school age. The power of his influence upon this family is identified as centering upon his youthful curiosity. Although the reading involves other family members, considerable information was directed toward the relationships between Robert, Terri, and Beau which has aided the smaller family unit.

The following excerpt begins by focusing on the mother of the family, Lorraine. The influence of her way of thinking is apparent in the attitudes of her children David and Connie as they approach adolescence.

"We see within the present period of time that once again the one referred to as Lorraine has a sense of jealousy towards these ones in which this one wants to have the strongest influence upon them. We see that there is a need for this one to come to terms with the more honest use of this one's own power and to release these ones in this one's own thinking to make their own decisions and go about their own way. We see for all of these ones, once again, to base most of their values around their physical gains. We see that each one will forsake and compromise principles to be able to have materially what they want, or what they see would give them the most selfishly at any given time.

We see that, once again, the ones referred to as David and Connie do have a greater curiosity in the understanding of higher ideals; and we see for these ones many times to recognize wrong attitudes and moves upon the part of the rest of the family. We see, however, that these ones do not usually stand up for their own principles, either with their family members or in the rest of their life and will still go along with the crowd. Would suggest to these two to begin building up some strength and some bravery, to make a stand for what they do believe in and to live by what they believe in, instead of going along with others when this goes against the beliefs of these two. We see, once again, there is a communication between them that could be very good for these two. We see, however, by the communication they do have that many times they will use it to relieve some of their pressure and then not take action on what they need to take action on. We see that as a whole there is need for this family to learn a greater sense of principles and values based

> *around the individual and the gains of the individual that are*
> *more than physical, but that would deal with a greater sense*
> *of morality and a greater sense of understood experiences*
> *and integrity." (4-2-86-1-CSR)*

It seems that everyone desires to have enjoyment, fulfillment, growth and learning in their life. To waste is a mistake for it slows learning. When nearing death, most people's regrets about their lives are for those things they have not done. When opportunities for sharing, giving and communication are passed over or avoided, the individual always gets hurt for they miss out on the learning.

Whatever the difficulty, communication can be an aid to enhance learning. Communication, however, is a two way street. It involves both talking and listening on the part of all parties concerned. Any organization, group, family, or structure of people is to be used for the individual's learning and growth for this is why we exist on the physical plane. When we can share our thoughts and activities with others of like minds our experiences on earth are more pleasant and often more rewarding. The family unit remains the cornerstone of our physical existence in one lifetime. Our early interactions with family members lay the foundation for the values we will hold, the dreams we will envision and the inner security to live those dreams. Family Readings uncover these productive elements of association and free family members to see themselves and each other in a new light.

Mental Heredity

There is a third important facet of Family Readings. This part consists of the specific questions the family may have, both about the past lifetime related and about the present. The body of the reading is complete since it is designed to give the information most needed and useful for the soul growth of each individual in the group. Yet many have questions of a specific nature, and any question revolving around the past or present which concerns family members can be asked.

To illustrate the wealth and variety of information available through the use of a Family Reading, consider these excerpts. Each give a glimpse of the wide range of personal interest questions that are relative to the information available in this kind of reading. First, questions concerning the past lifetime association are noted, then the Reader's response:

•Do you find this family to have an understanding of the workings of mind?
"The two men did develop some understanding of reasoning and related workings of the mind."

Did any of these entities have a formal education?
"All of them did."

Do you find any of them involved in the fine arts in creative artistic abilities?
"Only in the ways described."

What seemed to be the common goal that brought this family together during that lifetime?
"Wealth was needed to be learned by each of these as it was a common desire as well."

Were there unresolved situations that were not satisfied in the family during that time?
"Only desires that were not completely fulfilled."

Some questions pertain to unified pursuits during the past lifetime association, such as the following.

•Do you find this family to have been involved in the religious activities of that time and area?
"We see for the father to have been Catholic and to have followed this fairly closely. We see that religion was something that was private to him and although the wife was born Catholic, there was not really much

attention which she gave to it until the marriage."

The kind of religion followed in the past life is a common question that often aids family members in understanding their present day religious preferences or lack thereof. A family may have been Jewish in the past lifetime given and Catholic in the present lifetime. They have been Moslem or Hindu in the past and are Christian this lifetime.

People also derive insight from the identification of talents and skills demonstrated in the past life. Many times they discover these have a bearing on the present-day preferences for career choice or hobbies. They can also be a source of stimulation for latent abilities that can be brought forward and used in the present lifetime.

•Do you find any of these entities delving into painting or sculpting?
"We see for the father to be very artistic in the use of really any medium. We see for the youngest daughter to have talents as well. We see that the son was very good at drawing and was very good at designs and plans as well. He was not as skilled in painting."

The writing the mother did, was this involved in the business in any way?
"No."

Did the writing ever become published?
"There was one book that became published which was a combination of poems that this one had written."

How would this book be referred to at the present time?
"It is not in print at the present time. We see it referred to as Those of the Lost Soul."

Questions can also be asked concerning the present-day relationships between family members. These often reveal the essence of strong affinities or uncover deep-seated conflicts. The responses are directed to the family members in question and often information is given concerning how these members impact the remainder of the family.

> •The one of Lyn Lou asks the question, why is there friction between herself and the one referred to as Len?
> *"We see for this to be due to some lack of receptivity where there is not a knowing of the complete facts, and we see that it is mostly stemming from incomplete communication."*

> She also asks the question, why are we not a close-knit family?
> *"Because each one has difficulty in using situations or people to learn with."*

> What karmic debt links us together as a family and how can we rise above it?
> *"It is the karmic debt of each one individually to establish their own will power to use it productively. It is also common with each individual in the family that there is a need for self-control and self-discipline. By developing these qualities and skills individually this would aid in using the family unit to a greater extent."*

> What are the individual destinies for this lifetime?
> *"Whatever these ones choose it to be."*

> What are the souls' goals for this life?"
> *"The goals are to be realized and said in the conscious mind. The complete answer won't be given for this question."*

In this last question, the reason the souls' goals would not be given is the respect for the potential learning associated with causing the Self to discover the answer to this question. In readings involving past lifetimes, occasionally the person requesting the reading will ask a question which is not directly answered. When this occurs, however, the reply will revolve around potential actions the querent can pursue to reveal the answer to Self.

Many questions center on suggestions for greater familial understanding and harmony:

•Why are these ones not happy and fulfilled?
"They are to the extent they have been able to cause it."

Are there suggestions for bringing harmony into this family?
"To show more respect for each other's choices, more honest and open communication. These are the primary factors."

Are there suggestions for the one of Peter as to how to set goals and act on them?
"We see that it is the setting of goals where this one needs to learn more. We see that this one knows how to follow through or to be determined with goals when he does have one. This does not mean he always does it, but he does know how and there is a need for this effort. This is what will cause the difference in his thinking to pay off and will be something of use to him."

From these reading question and answer excerpts, you can see the large variety of information that is available. Questions that may have been troubling the family for years can be answered. The reading will show the reason these problems exist and suggestions for their relief.

One of the questions concerned the family's karmic debt to each other. Karma is defined as indebtedness as an individual. That is, the debt you owe to yourself to learn and grow to become a whole, functioning Self. A whole, functioning Self is a person who is using all parts of Self fully drawing upon present and past understandings to reach his full potential. A Family Reading is a tool to aid the individuals within the family to reach their full potential.

The question of the manner of death (withdrawal) was also discussed. The readings refer to death as withdrawal, meaning the attention is withdrawn from the conscious mind back into the subconscious mind. The subconscious mind is where you reside between lifetimes.

Questions were asked concerning creative abilities of the members of the family in the past lifetime. These individuals may have dormant understandings of art, music, and creativity that are just waiting to be expressed given the right stimulus. When asked if any special gifts or talents other than those mentioned in the early part of a reading could be elaborated upon, the response was full-bodied:

> *"We see there are many. We see upon the part of the one presently referred to as Tonya for there to be keen insights that this one has. We see for this one to be clairvoyant. We see for there to be many instances where this one can perceive probabilities of future events. We see that this one is excellent with organization and this one can work with people and cause there to be the meeting of compatible needs.*
>
> *We see upon the part of the one presently referred to as Debora for there to be a high degree of sensitivity that this one has developed to the needs of others and we see for this one to have the skill of listening. We see that this is well developed when this one wants to use it. This one does not always choose to do so.*
>
> *We see upon the part of Avram that there is once again the ability to be very focused, to be concentrated. We see capabilities for discrimination in terms of being able to identify what will work and what will not work.*
>
> *We see upon the part of the one presently referred to as Anna, that there is the nurturing capabilities that have already been described and the ability to embrace whatever this one puts the attention upon, whether this is a person, or a skill, something physical.*
>
> *We see upon the part of the one presently referred to as Charles that there is the capability of great problem solving,*

ofreasoning. We see that this one can be very strong in terms of holding the attention upon one thing for any extended period of time. This one can be very determined.

We see that all of these ones have a kind of artistic flair in that they do express themselves creatively. There are ways which each one of them do utilize things in creative ways. They are different and they are not necessarily noticed by themselves but there has been some communication between them concerning this." (5-25-91-3-BGO)

With this family individual talents as well as those in common were described. Of the many different types of questions that can be asked during a reading, those which are deeply considered, honestly drawn, and sincerely asked will bring the greatest insight and joy when answered.

During Family Readings, questions are asked in order to aid the family in understanding their relationship to each other. Often the results are surprising, even shocking. Some Family Readings, by relating the individual causal factor of the attitudes of family members, explain the reason why members of a family have similar diseases. Thoughts are things and all cause, including dis-ease, begins with a thought. As children are being raised by their parents, they will usually be taught the habits and unproductive thinking of their parents as well as the productive experiences. These unproductive thought patterns over time can create disorder within the physical body. Thus, diseases that are said to be inherited are often inherited more mentally than physically. Sometimes the attitudes passed down from one generation to another leads to similar disease from a parent to son or from a daughter to grandchild. This family asked a question as to why most of these entities suffer from sinus difficulties.

"There is such secrecy of those things which they love and those things which they hold sacred for fear that if they express them they will lose them. This is the attitude and the restriction within their own spirit that causes the physical difficulty in sinuses as well as some construction within the breathing and the air passages within the lungs....By using

what was suggested in this information about expressing themselves and their dreams and those things which they love and hold sacred this can change. (By) expressing these, they will find that they will not lose them but that these things will begin to become real in their lives and it will also release the restriction within the bodies that they express as this difficulty that they speak of." (2-9-87-1-CSR)

The exciting and fascinating answer given here opens a new area of understanding of family held diseases. Previously it was thought that these diseases were physically hereditary. We now find that some, if not many of them, are created from attitudes passed down from parents to children through generations. By breaking the chain of unproductive attitudes and by teaching individual family members to be more productive in their thinking and attitudes, the chain of cause is changed.

A reading for a mother and her two adult daughters included a question concerning the physical health of one of the daughters, Karen. Karen, who was adopted, has cerebral palsy. The mother asked for suggestions that might help all three of them to better cope with this disorder. The response is enlightening as it reveals the karmic nature of the daughter's condition.

"Would suggest first, to the other two it would be important for these ones to realize that they have not caused this disorder and therefore in that way are not responsible for it. If this is understood, then there can be a freedom in the choices made according to what these two want to give to the one of the other. It would be important for these ones to remember that whatever they do choose to offer is something that is given because they so desire and this would be the idea to keep uppermost in mind.

Upon the part of the one presently referred to as Karen, we see that this is at a stage where this one could adjust the attitudes to such a way as to cause there to be a difference in the ways that it manifests and even a change in the quality and caliber of the physical strength. We see that this one is very strong-willed and therefore this is a great asset in this one being able to cause there to be a change in this disorder.

> *We see that the will, however, has been allowed to be stubborn rather than directed by intelligence and thereby will-power. This one has many available opportunities to express the intelligence she holds and we see that with the discipline and directed use of the intelligence there could be great changes effected. This would need to be a desire upon this one's part, however, for as in the past lifetime related, this one has fought discipline throughout the life, and there would need to be a change in this. It is because of the fighting in part that this one has manifested this disorder in the life. It is therefore a challenge for this one to meet, and the challenge is no greater than this one is." (5-23-91-18-BGO)*

One Family Reading was given for a family composed of a husband, wife, and three daughters. At the time of the reading all five were adults. The husband-father in the present time period was about to die, or what is referred to in readings as "withdraw from the physical". In talking with one of the daughters, I learned she was very happy to have received this reading before her father died. She used the information to understand and come to terms with many aspects of her family and her growing up years that would not have been possible otherwise.

The woman knew that we do not do readings on someone who has withdrawn from the physical. Our duty is to aid the people in the physical to become whole, functioning Selves. The physical is the place you build permanent understandings that you carry with you from lifetime to lifetime. Because the reading was timely for the conditions in this family, the daughter continues to have this information about her past to aid her in being more productive in the present long after her father's death.

Although a family member who is no longer alive cannot be included in the Family Reading, significant information has been gained concerning the living family member's attitudes about a death in the family. A reading for a mother and her children did not include her recently deceased husband, but a question asked provided significant insight into the husband/father's relationship with the family both from the past lifetime and the present. It offered insight to the children concerning their father's death:

"We see in the past lifetime related this one that has been queried (the husband/father) was the mother in concern that has been described. The experience of the ones presently referred to as Angelique and Catharina was very similar to the one in the past lifetime related where there was the kinds of distances for the reasons that have already been stated. We see that in the present time period there is a similar kind of attitude that these ones have. In part it is a kind of distance that they experience now, a kind of definiteness of finality, a kind of yearning for something that cannot occur, a kind of desire for communication which they feel has been thwarted - at least this is true for the one of Angelique - or a kind of apathy or giving up in what they do desire to change. (There is the impression that what) they would have desired cannot now occur. Would suggest that upon each one of these parts that this is not so, that these ideas that have been described are stimuli for these ones to think more completely, to cause there to be understanding brought into their existence so that they themselves can be different and the relationships that they have in their life can be different. Would suggest that it be looked at in this way.

Would suggest also that the reality of their existence is not quite as final as these ones would see it and there is still the available opportunity for communication, that there is still the openness for learning and for exchange of love. Would suggest that these ones recognize that whatever is given in this way with intention does fulfill a purpose and it is a reality that these ones can experience." (5-23-91-18-BGO)

Through the many years of providing readings, I have repeatedly discovered and been reminded of their unlimited value, not only for the people immediately receiving the reading but for anyone who is invested in the progression of their soul. The insights from this reading concerning the understanding of life and death are universally applicable and can be useful to anyone. When studied as a body of research material, Family Readings also reveal the universal threads which form the bonds of giving and receiving between independent souls.

Each individual and every family has the right and duty to understand who they are, where they came from, where they are going, why they have chosen to incarn with a specific family, and where and when have they been with this family before. Family readings may present past life associations in such varied places and time periods as France in the 1700's, England in the 1600's, China in 1100's, Egypt 500 B.C., India 700 B.C., Peru in 500 A.D, or Atlantis in 10,000 B.C. Each past life association from a Family Reading will have its own time period and location. You can explore real history, not one the historians have recorded from their point of view, rather one relative to you and your family's past life history.

During his pursuit of a Masters degree in agricultural economics from the University of Missouri, travels in Central America, South America, and Western Europe enabled Daniel Condron to study diverse cultures and lifestyles. An author, teacher, and counselor, Dr. Daniel completed all levels of study offered through the School of Metaphysics earning his Doctorate in Metaphysics. For years, he has aided thousands of people by serving as a Conductor of the readings offered by SOM and by training many of the individuals who give readings.

Serving globally as a teacher of mind and spirit, Dr. Daniel has shared his knowledge and research with thousands through formal study, seminars, and conferences. His major address on "Permanent Healing - Breakthrough to Awareness" *was warmly received at the 1993 Parliament of the World's Religions in Chicago. He serves as an international spokesman for the National Dream Hotline®, appearing on radio from London to Hong Kong. He has written several books including* Permanent Healing, The Universal Language of Mind: The Book of Matthew Interpreted, *and* Dreams of the Soul: The Yogi Sutras of Patanjali. *He is currently writing books on meditation and the* "Book of Revelation".

A Who'sWho biographee, Dr. Daniel serves as president of the board of directors of the School of Metaphysics and is chancellor of the College of Metaphysics.   He lives on campus with his wife Barbara and their son Hezekiah.

Part II
The Health Analyses

About the Health Analysis....

"The accuracy of the reading is quite amazing. The insights into my mental and emotional states are challenging and the suggestions for improvement are inspiring. Studying the reading has quickened the desire in me to work on these issues." — Sheldon Heckman, Christiansted, St. Croix, U.S.V.I.

"The health reading I had done at the end of January '91 was invaluable to me and you have my deepest gratitude. According to traditional medicine, I was in 'perfect' health. What was wrong with me didn't show up on their tests and I felt total despair. After receiving the reading, I was at last relieved to know what needed fixing..I have been seeing (a specialist) for a year now and am a 'new' person today." — Linda Ordogh, Westmount, Quebec, Canada

"I just wanted to write and thank you for my recent health reading. I had been very sick and your reading really helped me to work on the problem from both a spiritual and physical vantage point. And it helped greatly to relieve a lot of my fears. I can't thank you enough for providing this wonderful service."
                                                    — Barbara Lewis, Waggaman, Louisiana

"....Then came a period where I started getting dizzy spells, vague aches and pain and headaches, which was a rare event for me. I went to my doctor which then must have charged the insurance company a few thousand dollars for a battery of tests to find the nature of my illness. The doctor had originally stated to me jokingly that I was either dying or that I was under a great amount of stress. Well, all the tests came back negative. So what was wrong with me?

My fellow meteorologist and metaphysical friend advised me to ask the School of Metaphysics for a health reading, which I did. My first reaction to the reading was one of disappointment, since no physical problem could be found here either. It was mentioned however that I should not be subjecting myself to so much strain.

So I stated my disappointment to my friend and he told me that he and his wife had never heard of a reading that was so brief. Then he allowed me to listen to a reading that he had gotten and was it lengthy. It told where he had a designated vertebrae in his lower neck that was misaligned, and he had me feel that spot and indeed it was. After explaining to me how accurate the other comments had been, I reevaluated my reading, finding it to say more than I had originally heard, and decided that indeed here also was a good reading since it reaffirmed what my doctor had surmised after thousands of dollars worth of tests, that I was under a great amount of stress. Since my job had just been abolished with new duties reassigned whole being in the middle of a massive reorganization going on and doing all of this while working 24 hour around the clock rotation shift work, maybe I was stressed out without really knowing it. Yes, now I was impressed.

continued on page 112

The First Wealth

Over a century ago, American poet, essayist, and philosopher Ralph Waldo Emerson wrote "the first wealth is health." How aptly stated for man's existence! For what use can we make of our potential, the loves in our lives, the possessions we garner in the physical world, the acclaim and awards our accomplishments may bring, if good health escapes us?

The keen observer and participant in life will earnestly seek ways to cause good health, rather than wait for debilitating disease to take hold of the mind and body before health producing change is caused. Learning what causes health insures wealth for any Thinker, for the principles that cause health are the same principles the mind uses to insure wealth.

In today's world the connection between the mind and body is well known and accepted. Mental and emotional stress are often cited as initiators and contributors to diseases in the body. However, the mechanics of how thinking occurs and how specific thoughts cause specific parts of the body to function or malfunction is not common knowledge.

Today's physician finds his day filled by demands that he practice his well-developed skills of alleviating pain by eradicating diseased tissue through surgical removal or scientific destruction. This does not lend itself easily to the investigation or instruction of what will cause prolonged health.

Long gone seem the days when the family doctor made it his business to know the loves and hates, dreams and fears of everyone in the family, as well as making himself available for the immediate physical treatment life experiences might require. Ahead of his time, he used what was at hand, natural foods and herbs to stimulate balance in the physical body. The family doctor of a century ago may not have had the benefits of science to support him, but he did have his experiences and the attention of the mind to aid him with each patient. Now we are discovering in our rush for physical comfort, we have sacrificed the knowledge of what will cause long-term health with our demands for a quick cure.

For anyone determined to possess a sound mind and healthy body, the Health Analyses are a revealing and reliable source of information. Readers are trained to use the deepest level of the subconscious mind to report the states of consciousness producing disease in three systems of the whole Self. Since these readings are obtained in the innermost, third level of the subconscious mind, specific ways of thinking are described which affect the emotions and eventually the physical body. Armed with this knowledge, the person receiving the analysis can use the suggestions for change given in the analysis to cause immediate symptomatic relief in the body and permanent relief through adjusting mental and emotional attitudes. Once the origin of a problem is known, admitted, and changed, the individual can insure his continued good health.

Health Analyses have given the cause and needed changes for every type of disorder. A woman has tried to become pregnant for years and finds significant guidance in her reading for producing the manifestation of her desires. An analysis detects a heart murmur in an unsuspecting man which is later confirmed when, under medication for oral surgery, the heart begins to oscillate irregularly causing alarm in the operating room. Why an autistic child often causes abuse to his body is revealed to be the way the child is attempting to understand fear by startling the Self into using his senses. A Conductor of the readings becomes perturbed by the seeming interference of a gentleman during a woman's reading until it is discovered that the man is not only the woman's husband but also her doctor and he understands what the analysis is revealing more than anyone else present. A man is perplexed when the Reader examines his thyroid which he believed was medically removed years before until further tests confirm that one third of the gland had been left, purposefully, by his doctor. When using a controlled and directed use of the subconscious mind the picture of total health becomes known.

Although the mind and body have a universal structure, each individual treats and uses his mind and body in his own unique way. By studying Health Analyses many universals can be discerned, yet each reading is as unique as the fingerprints of the individual being examined. Thus, precise suggestions for change in each person is given in the body of the reading. For instance, an individual suffers from digestive disorders including stomach ulcers and colon congestion. Suggestions for symptomatic relief include acidophilus milk or buttermilk which will serve as relief for both conditions rather than fibrous fruit juices that would stimulate the colon but aggravate the ulcerous condition.

In this section, Sheila Benjamin gives you an intimate look into the needs and benefits of Health Analyses for the individual. The experimental nature of these readings, developed through years of research, reveals startling connections between specific ways of thinking and their corresponding physical disorders as well as document man's ability to create health.

The skill that reveals what will produce health in an individual, is also used to examine what will produce health in a group of individuals. This can be gained in the Business Analyses offered by the School of Metaphysics. The Business Analysis reports the mental and emotional conditions in a group of minds that create disorder in the "body" commonly called a business. As with the individual Health Analysis, identifying and changing disorders where they begin frees the outer, physical workings of the vehicle examined. That vehicle can be one individual's physical body or a common vehicle such as a business that is used by many people.

From embezzling to gas leaks in a building, from where oil can be found in a piece of property to the advantages or disadvantages of company mergers, from attitudes of employees to attitudes of clients or customers, Business Analyses give information and suggestions to enhance productivity and profits rarely found in other types of analyses available. What some specialists take months to discern and charge the business owners thousands of dollars to research can be gained within an hour for a minimal financial investment through using the service of a Business Analysis. Laurel Jan Clark examines this exceptional use of intuitive skill which places any business on the cutting edge of success.

For those who have taken health out of the hands of fate or destiny and placed it into their own hands as a matter of choice, this section will enhance your beliefs in your ability to master your own good health and fortune.

..Lastly I'll tell you about a lady meteorologist that we worked with. She was impressed about our stories of Health Readings and decided to get one for herself. However, considering herself a scientist, she was skeptical. So she asked for a reading but intentionally neglected to mention her lifelong respiratory problem. She said she didn't want to give you leading information, and that this was to be her 'ace in the hole' to prove your validity. Then when she started reading the information you sent her, she felt tears come into her eyes as the reading zeroed in on this very problem. 'How could you have known about this?' she wondered. I know she was no longer skeptic and she developed a love for metaphysics...."
— Anthony Loriso, Clinton, Maryland

"I had a very helpful health reading from you last October. The suggestions, most of which I followed, gave me quite a lot of relief. I was surprised at the suggestion to drink 'whole milk', but followed it and found it great for ridding me of phlegm and bowel waste. The 'goals' I needed to seek have led me to school, where I am presently taking pre-requisite courses for nursing school but I am hesitant, I find my heart not in it because I love tending plants which is what I do now for a living. Thus this request for a life reading. I am grateful you are available, and I thank you and God for the help."
— Frances Grove, Phoenix, Arizona

"I was more than pleased with the accuracy of the reading. I want to thank you for helping me mentally, emotionally, and physically. The advice (about an itchy eye problem) that was given to me from my reading proved to be very helpful. My eye condition has improved immensely."
— Christine McGinty, Las Vegas, Nevada

"...I am prepared to make two general observations about the readings:
1) The approach is holistic, combining psychological, physiological, and spiritual factors in a manner which orients the subject toward increasing his state of well-being rather than merely focusing on disease care. I strongly approve of this approach. 2) The analysis of the spinal condition as given by the reading was consistent with the clinical X-ray findings."
— Mark Genero, D.C., Ann Arbor, Michigan

"You recently did a Health Analysis Reading for me that was truly awesome. The depth and value of the information received was superior. It spoke of truths that only my soul could know and I was in awe of the accuracy. The message was so well-spoken as well. I am grateful to you for this service as I feel certain it will aid in bringing in more light to go higher and help me through some of the issue I have been dealing with. I am delighted to help spread the word about your service. Thank you!" — Sharla Hawkins, Aurora, Colorado

"The mind has great influence
over the body, and maladies often
have their origin there."
—*Moliere (1665)*

Health Analyses
by Sheila Benjamin, B.A., D.M.

Thoughts are Things

I first heard about the School of Metaphysics when a friend from college arranged for a Health Analysis to be done for me as a birthday gift. Deborah knew about the reading consultations because she had been taking classes at the center in Chicago. I had seen many changes in her expression during that time. She appeared to be softer, more loving. She was calmer and had come to terms with the anger she had carried for many years. When I asked Deborah what was going on, she said she was learning about how thoughts manifest in the physical world. I asked her how long she planned on taking courses at the School and she replied, "Until I get my Doctorate." All I could do was mentally roll my eyes because I knew Deborah's tendency to move from one stimulating venture to another. But now I was receiving a Health Analysis from that School.

I wasn't physically present when my reading was done although I was aware of the time it was scheduled. In my imagination I could see this woman in a trance-like state in a room filled with other people. I knew there was no way Deborah could have told the Reader anything about me because the Reader was arriving in Chicago that day. I was skeptical, but game for the experience. Not being present for the reading eased any apprehensions I had.

I noted what was going on in my world at the time the reading was to take place so I could verify any information that was given. I was unsure of this whole experience wanting to see if these people would give useful insight. At the time of the reading, I was at my place of employment working with a woman who was very scattered. She would appear very busy but accomplish little. Because of her tunnel vision, I had to work twice as hard so my day was frustrating and I had a very large headache.

Later that day I listened to the cassette tape of my reading. This is how it began:

> *"This one is feeling quite annoyed at this point. We do see her reacting very spontaneously to the point where she can become easily motivated, stimulated, or annoyed. We see this one quite impatient at this point. We see a certain amount of disdain for the activity at hand, and this one is feeling unappreciated and not particularly enjoying what she is doing. We see her to feel restricted in her freedom at this time and does not feel satisfied. We see there is a need for this one to use the present activity as a stepping stone to something higher or better within her own recognition. As long as she is resenting it she is not getting any betterment from it.*

> *We do see that there is a need for a formulation of a goal for herself, for we see her to be living from day-to-day without any sense of purpose. We do see that if she were then to formulate a goal, and use whatever activity at hand there is to create a respect for self in achieving that goal, she can more efficiently experience life.*

> *We see this one feels some resentment towards another individual at this time. In fact, there are several. This one becomes angry when she feels that others are not agreeing with her ideals and yet she is not really clear on what her ideals are. We do see that there is a desire for experiencing harmony in all situations and she tends to take it very personally when there is not total agreement at all times. We do see that there is a part of herself that desires to express anger at these moments, but we do see that she will not give herself permission to express anger and thus there would be a tendency to hold inside self the annoyance she experiences and become involved in a self pity attitude."*

When I first heard this reading its accuracy shocked me. I knew there was something to these readings and this School because this woman had just revealed my innermost secrets. She was speaking thoughts only I knew I had because I had never told anyone. I had just moved back to Chicago having spent four structured years away at college, and now I didn't know what I wanted to do. She continued with the reading, describing physical conditions that I was experiencing in my digestive system and even describing what foods caused the most discomfort. I was convinced that there was a great deal of truth and value in these readings and in this organization. I at least began to consider the idea that there was truth to the mind and body connection.

Soon after receiving this reading, I began taking classes in the study of the mind at the School of Metaphysics. I wanted to learn how I could change some of those inharmonious attitudes and thoughts into ones that would cause me to feel joy and peace. I also wanted to experience something I felt very little – love. In the classes I learned that unexpressed thoughts of guilt, resentment or even indecisiveness produce physical diseases and disorders. I also learned how to correct those attitudes in myself as well as others. For there to be health and wholeness, thoughts need positive direction to cause forward motion. This was important to me because at the age of 22 I still experienced the acne condition I had had since entering puberty.

I had acne since the age of twelve. It seemed that when I reached puberty I constantly fought the blemishes that would erupt on my face. I was quite upset by this because my older sister had beautiful skin and I didn't understand why I should have acne. I didn't think it was fair. When I received my reading, I discovered how often I wanted to express anger but would not give myself permission to do so. This caused me to wonder when I first developed this self-defeating habit.

When I was about five years old, I decided I wouldn't cry. I created this strange pact with myself because my older sister cried enough for both of us. Being the middle child of three, I was looking for that special identity which belonged to only me. I wanted to feel special and be treated that way by adults. I felt a little lost as to how to gain the kind of attention I wanted, having noted that my father wasn't too impressed with my older sister's crying spells. He would say, "Stop your crying" or "I'll give you something to cry about." I knew he would never hit my sister, but her constant crying grated on his nerves.

I looked up to my father. He was very strong emotionally and I knew he wore the pants in the house because when he spoke I and everyone else heeded his words. He wasn't a cuddly dad, one that easily expresses his warmth and loving side, but he was so very strong in my eyes I never felt lost around him. I decided I wanted to be "Daddy's little girl" but because of my dad's character I had my work cut out for me.

I began to imitate him, and that meant I did not cry about anything. Many times I wanted to cry either from pain or fear, but I resolved I would not. I just swallowed those feelings and never complained. I was good at pretending, but I began to get sick a lot.

I always had sore throats or fever blisters. My mother became very concerned because I also tired easily. Every Saturday, I visited the doctor for blood tests trying to determine just what was wrong with me. When I moved into adolescence, I grew out of sore throats and fever blisters into a face of blemishes. The older I got, the worse it became. I went to several different doctors who treated me in all kinds of ways, but nothing seemed to improve my condition. I began to withdraw further and further into myself. When I received my reading, this was one of the areas I asked about and this was the response:

> *"There is an uneven distribution of oils in the skin to where there are areas that are extremely dry and other areas that are extremely oily. We do see this creating blemishes. We do see the uneven distribution relates to the involvement of the nervous system and the tendency to not allow self to speak her opinions, to hold back in this way. This can be altered by utilizing the suggestions already given especially in formulating a goal and allowing self to be stimulated each day by focusing on this goal. As this one then works in the physical in evening out the attitudes, the periods of enthusiasm, the periods of slowed reaction, as those become evened out, the body functioning will balance out as well. Then there will be a more even distribution of body energies, fluids, oils, and such." (6-5-78-8-JMW)*

In the section of my reading I quoted earlier, the Reader spoke about the anger I had kept inside, refusing to express it outwardly. This seemed to make sense to me since I described myself as being very shy.

Even though I had opinions, I very rarely expressed them to others. Some of my first thoughts went back to when I was a child and I refused to cry because I wanted to be strong. I learned this refusal to express thoughts from watching my older sister cry about everything. Even though she received a great deal of attention, the attention she received was not pleasant from my point of view. I also watched my dad. He seemed always to be in control, never looking sad or hurt, although he did raise his voice in anger. Even though I loved my father, he would scare me when he yelled, so I tried to be as good as I could to avoid his wrath.

I can look back now on my childhood and see why I had manifested the various conditions I did. When I was about five I started refusing to express my thoughts, feelings, and emotions. I began to experience herpes coupled with a high fever, making me delirious. From that time forward I created phobias attached to the world around me. I was afraid of birds, dogs, horses, even the wind. My world changed because I held onto strong thoughts of no longer being in control of me or my life.

When I was seven, the sore throats began. At that time no one around me knew that this disorder arises from a weak use of will or the need to follow through on a decision that has been made. At seven, my family was planning to move and I was not sure I wanted this to happen. I knew I had no choice in the matter but that didn't keep me from being very upset about the friends I was leaving behind. My world was changing and I had no choice in the matter.

With the onset of adolescence, my face was in full bloom, covered with blemishes. Even though I was a few years older, I still had not learned to express my thoughts. I was extremely shy and would not look people in the eyes. I had very little respect for my self or my ideas because I wasn't sure if others would see things in the way I did, or if my ideas were right, so I just kept to myself.

When I received my first Health Analysis, it gave me permission in a sense to begin expressing my thoughts and feelings, getting ideas and emotions out of my head so I could begin to experience calmness within. This did take some time because I was at least 22 years of age before I began speaking my mind. I received another reading about a year later. By this time the blemishes were beginning to calm down but there were still scars on my face marking the presence of those old attitudes. I asked what could be done about this and the Reader stated that I needed to begin loving myself realizing thoughts which I viewed as wrong were not a reflection of my worth and value. The reading suggested I spend time looking at my reflection in the mirror and project loving thoughts to my self. As symptomatic relief, an application of baking soda and lemon juice paste was suggested to assist the release of toxins from my skin.

Since that time I have made great changes in my ability to express myself. I learned that anger was not something evil, rather an indication of a need for understanding. Most importantly I have learned to love and respect myself. My world looks much brighter now and in my control. The Health Reading I received began my search for truth within Self and within the world. Since that time, discoveries and learning in the field of health and healing now enable me to live, display, and teach others a more productive way to live.

The Three-Fold Nature of Health Analyses

A Health Analysis can be a tool for inspiration as well as accurate information for self-evaluation. Many times it is easier to be objective about others than it is to be objective about ourselves. We tend to get involved in ourselves and our experiences, forgetting the bigger picture of life as souls having a connection with our Creator. Because Health Analyses describe the mental and emotional disorders, they offer this type of objective viewpoint. The mental disorders cited are ways of thinking which are out of alignment with our true nature. The emotional disorders described will show how these misunderstandings are expressed outwardly. To gain the full benefit from a Health Analysis, you must consider that the mind has the capability of chang-ing. Because we as thinkers can change our identity, we can also change our mental and emotional states as well as our physical bodies. These changes are created through the use of imagination, will and reasoning.

A Health Analysis examines the health aura to give a complete analysis of the mental, emotional, and physical state of the individual requesting the reading. The physical body, as well as thoughts, emanate an expression of energy. This is called an aura. When we have a thought, be it productive or not, energy is used in giving that thought life. Scientists tell us that nothing is made new and nothing is destroyed, only changed in appearance. All matter is energy in the process of change.

Our auras are a result of energy changing from its grossest point, the physical expression, back to its more subtle and finer form of the origin of thought. For this reason the Reader's attention is directed to the deepest level of the subconscious mind where thoughts begin. The Reader then describes the health of the person requesting the reading. Beginning with the causal disorders in the thinking, these are traced through their emotional expression and, finally, the resulting condition of the physical body. The Reader is also instructed to relate suggestions for the correction of any disorder seen.

The body of the reading is separated into three components. The first portion is the examination of any mental attitudes or thought disorders including suggestions for causing more harmony in the thinking. This section gives the client a way to see what he can do to change his patterns of thinking and lifestyle to produce health. For example, in my first reading which I have shared with you I wanted to know how to correct the condition with my skin. The acne was the effect in the physical of my mental attitudes of feeling worthless and not expressing my thoughts or opinions. These attitudes caused a distortion in the normal patterns of communication between my mind and the physical nerve impulses in my body. As I used the suggestions given and began to express my thoughts without attachment to whether others would agree, my skin began to heal.

The second portion of a Health Analysis focuses on the emotional system relating how the individual uses or misuses the expression of these energies and again suggestions for using the emotions more productively are offered. My reading noted that I expressed much through the emotions often draining my Self of energy by extreme mood changes from one moment to the next. By failing to fully express my thoughts, my body would at one point be full of energy, ready to fight, and then fatigued. The reading stated that until I could change my thinking and begin to use that energy with direction, I would need periods of rest in order to heal my body.

The final portion of the analysis examines the physical body of the client describing any primary disorder seen. Suggestions for symptomatic relief through diet, herbs, vitamins, and exercise are given as well as suggestions for care from health professionals when needed. These recommendations are for temporary, physical relief giving the client time to make changes in the thinking patterns where the disorders originate. All the conditions that an individual may be experiencing are considered and suggestions for correction are given. For instance, one woman was experiencing inflammation in the duodenum and small intestine, as well as fluctuations in blood sugar levels. Her reading suggested ingesting small amounts of lemon water and adding foods with alkaline content to aid in digestion. Jerusalem artichokes were suggested for greater utilization of sugars and red meat for increased levels of iron in the blood. These recommendations were for temporary, physical relief giving the woman time to make changes in the thinking patterns where her disorders began.

The value of these analyses lies in what they can teach you about cause and effect. The information is presented so you can trace the physical conditions back to mental and emotional disorders. You can use the suggestions to cause not only temporary healing but also permanent healing. When you change attitudes from disorder to order, you cause health in your physical body. This state of health produces a permanent healing. Physical substances such as vitamins, herbs, and prescription drugs can temporarily relieve the pain or even eliminate the problem, however unless there is a change in the thinking the offending condition will reoccur.

To be whole and healthy, one must have mental, emotional, and physical well-being. According to an ancient definition by Pericles, health is "that state of moral, mental, and physical well-being which enables a man to face any crisis in life with the utmost facility and grace." The following analysis is an example of this ancient idea.

> *"Would suggest to this one that health is not only physical. Health does begin within this one's own outlook upon life. It is in this one considering the Self to be very beautiful, very worthwhile and deserving of living a very beautiful, worthy life. This would initiate the action that would produce health within the entire system"* (7-25-90-6-LJF)

Through information gained in Health Analyses, you can begin making connections between the mental thoughts and the physical conditions you are experiencing. The following excerpt was for a man who displayed a great deal of patience with others while being very hard on himself. It describes how a restriction in the ability to express feelings, especially emotional reactions which have been labeled as wrong, can cause disorders in the lungs. In essence, this man is suffocating himself by not being true to self and expressing who he is.

> *"We see within the emotional system there to be a type of depression that is taking place. Would suggest to this one that it is important for this one to express this one's feelings for we see that at the present time period the type of denial that this one is expressing is causing a slowness of this one's own expression. Would suggest as this one begins to express the emotions to recognize that the emotions that this one analyzes intellectually as being harmful to the self and to others can be useful in aiding this one to evaluate where this one is within this one's own thinking. We see that as a result of this suppression of emotions, this one experiences a great deal of strain within this one's physical body. We see there to be difficulty within the respiratory system and also an accumulation of phlegm. Would suggest that deep breathing would aid in strengthening this area, as well as the inhalation of steam which would aid in moistening and breaking down the phlegm." (2-14-91-5-SMR)*

Many people feel that the way to achieve emotional control is to suppress the emotions. They never wonder what happens to the energy when denied expression. If we place a knot in a garden hose to prevent water from moving through the hose, but never turn the water off, what do you think will eventually happen to the hose? The pressure from the water would eventually cause the hose to burst. The same thing happens to us when we continue to deny that we feel angry or hurt. Eventually, something will trigger us so we explode in an emotional outburst or if given no release, the explosion occurs in our physical body in the form of disease. This man's reading indicated his need to express his feelings so he could become more self aware. There are better ways than physical disease to understand your emotions and be in control of them.

Each Health Analysis is designed to identify any disorder whether mental, emotional, or physical. This gives clear insight into areas needing to be changed and corrected to create wholeness. These analyses are complete in and of themselves. During each analysis, the Conductor serves as a connecting link between you and the Reader. In addition to insuring accuracy and quality, the Conductor relates to the Reader the questions you may have concerning the information given. Since readings relate primary disorders, there may be secondary disorders that will not be addressed unless specific questions are asked. For example, the skin eruptions I was experiencing at the time of my first analysis were a secondary disorder stemming from the build-up of toxins caused by malfunction in my eliminatory system. Because some of the organs involved in elimination were not performing their function, my body was compensating, trying to find another route for the elimination of waste. My skin had become this vehicle for cleansing the body.

Another example of a secondary condition addressed in a Health Analysis concerns a woman who desired to know the cause of hives and how she could stop them.

> *"There are skin eruptions, but we do not see the condition referred to as 'hives'. We see that the skin eruptions are a reaction, a nervous reaction, to the amount of energy in the body that does not have an outlet to the condition of the nervous system that has been described." (7-11-89-5-BGO)*

A variety of questions can be answered with the use of the Health Analyses. A recent analysis addressed a woman's health in relation to her spiritual learning. She was a nurse who had been working with AIDS patients and who had become HIV positive through a needle-stick. Seeking counseling from a close friend who knew about the readings, her friend suggested she receive an analysis. The nurse wanted to know the purpose for this experience at this time in her life because she believed there was a spiritual lesson for her to learn. She was also curious about the karmic implications wondering if her condition had any relationship to past life debts. The reading offered this insight:

> *"We see this experience is a way for this one to change this one's perspective in helping people, not to stop helping them but that with a different perspective this one could be of much more help to this one's Self and to others. Would suggest to this one that this experience does not mean that this one's body is in a condition to fully deteriorate with the virus. There is a need for this one to stop these types of visualizations and to recognize that although this one has tested positive this one can carry this virus throughout this one's life without ever passing it onto another human being or manifesting symptoms in this one's own physical body.*
>
> *Would suggest to this one that it would only be through this one's own attitudes of sympathy and of fully identifying with those that this one is trying to help that this one could manifest the full conditions of that virus. It is a possibility this one could produce those circumstances in the life, but it is not needed. The producing of this experience has been through this one's too strong identification with this one's patients rather than identifying with this one's own learning and this one's own life. This one has become too emotionally involved where this one has lost this one's Self in this one's work and loved ones that are this one's patients.*
>
> *There is a need for this one to keep a sense of Self, yet have the compassion and involvement with others. This is the lesson in this experience for this one. This one can make it as easy or as difficult as this one chooses. It is not through punishment or anything that this one would need to be punished for that this experience is present. It really can be one that can change this one's life for the better."*

This information clarified the mental attitudes causing the nurse's physical condition. It answered her questions concerning the opportunity to learn and verified that her condition was not the result of some misdeed in a past lifetime. The karma, or indebtedness to Self, revolved around her need to learn about Self by adding to her understandings in the way described.

Since she intends to pursue health, the nurse specifically asked for guidance in Self healing. Having plans for marriage and children, her questions included these areas of concern. The analysis revealed that she could marry and carry a child without infecting her partner or the fetus with the virus. This would depend upon her attitudes and the actions she would take from this point forward. The reading offered the following guidance concerning the healing process:

> *"Would suggest to this one that just as many times a small amount of a poison is given to produce immunity, this one can cause this experience to occur in a similar manner. Whereby, the introduction of the virus into this one's system can be used and depending upon the way this one's own immune system acts on it this could produce immunity in this one's body toward the virus.*
>
> *We see besides the visualizing of this, the learning of Self worth, the learning of having a purpose for this one's own growth, a purpose of this one's own for serving others, would aid this one greatly as well. Primarily the change in attitude that would effect the change in this one's immune system would be for this one to be as free and as giving in a compassionate way as this one has been but through the elimination of this one's sympathizing. This one could be even more loving and compassionate for there is a certain place where this one's sympathy stops the Self from loving and caring. We see also that the sympathy causes this one to lose the sense of Self and causes this one to lose respect for the individuals this one works with. Therefore, changing the sympathy to compassion or empathy is much of what is occurring at the present period of time and is the learning that is needed. Would suggest to this one that the practicing and the learning of telepathy could also aid this one in making this change, and producing the understanding that this one desires to experience."* (5-29-90-6-CSR)

As described in this analysis, it is always our freedom to change our attitudes and cause health to be a part of our whole being.

All readings offered through the School of Metaphysics are recorded on cassette tape and given to the client. Health Analyses are an average of fifteen minutes of constant information that you can use for months and even years to enhance your health. Through the years, we have served people on six continents with Health Readings. You need not be physically present to receive this type of reading, but the complete address of where you will be at the time the reading is done is required.

Raising a Healthy Child

Anyone can receive a Health Analysis. Throughout the years, Health Analyses have been given for those with minor disorders and for the terminally ill, for those with medically diagnosed conditions and for those medical science fails to diagnose, for the elderly and for infants.

Parents are often concerned with raising their child in a healthy way. The Health Analysis is an excellent resource for parents because it offers insight for raising a healthy child based on the child's needs. Until the age of seven a child is like a sponge, absorbing thoughts and feelings from his environment. The parents, the siblings, and others of surrounding influence determine the attitudes the child forms in these early years. These attitudes formed early in life can influence the life of the growing adult to come. Once identified, attitudes which are productive can be built upon and those which are unproductive can be changed. The health is affected according to the attitudes received and held by the child.

Not long ago, a couple used the information gained in a Health Analysis to seek a cure for their daughter's health problem. At the age of four and a half years, their daughter Mary had yet to speak words. She only made sounds. At times the frustration she experienced due to this language barrier would show itself in angry temper tantrums. Mary would jump up and down, crying, yet no words accompanied her actions. Equally frustrated and concerned for their child's well-being, the parents did not know if Mary was mentally or physically disabled. Having had readings for themselves, the parents decided to pursue an analysis for Mary.

The reading described Mary's scattered attention which caused her to have difficulty effectively using her physical body. This inhibited the reception of information through her five senses. Recommendations were made directly to the parents with specific instruction to aid their child.

> *"It would be of benefit for those around this one to demand this one's attention. This would not be in regards to an emotional demand, but in regards to intentionally taking an object and placing it before this one, causing it to move, causing this one's attention to be drawn to it and held for periods of time. This could be accomplished through shapes, through colors, through sounds, through tactile experiences. This one needs to be drawn out in terms of this one's thinking and use of the body in the senses.*
>
> *We see that emotionally there is great frustration building, for this one is unable to communicate effectively this one's experiences. There is not the information stored or the ability to communicate effectively and this is beginning to build great frustration. Therefore there are times when this one will cry or throw tantrums in an effort to express this frustration. Would suggest that those surrounding this one should not misinterpret this with their own imagination, but should recognize it for what it is and begin to teach this one what is needed in order for the types of communication that would be of greater benefit to this one and those around this one to occur."*

This information aided Mary's parents in beginning to understand why she was not talking. She had a difficult time receiving information completely to learn communication skills. However, the cause for this interruption was still not clear. Mary's parents asked specifically why their child was not yet talking and if there was any physiological damage that was interfering with the ability to use the senses properly.

> *"We see that part of this is due to incomplete information being stored and the suggestion has been given in that regard. Part of it is due to the way that the nerves are*

*growing, particularly the function of the pituitary. We see
that there needs to be more minerals in this one's diet,
particularly manganese, zinc, potassium, and iron. We see
that the suggestions given to draw this one's attention out
and cause this one to focus will be of the greatest benefit
mentally, emotionally, and physically. There is also a need
for this one to learn how to use the mouth. Teaching
phonetics or diction could be of help.*

*We see there is some pushing together of the cranial plates,
particularly the crown of the head and the back of the skull.
We see that there is a slight swelling that occurs because of
the movement of the fluids in this area."* (2-21-89-14-BGO)

The pressure on the nerves caused partial reception of sensory information to the brain. Physiologically, Mary was handicapped by the mineral
deficiency and the cranial plates putting pressure on these nerves.

For over a year, the parents worked with the information
received to aid in the growth of their child. The mother worked with her
child in doing exercises that increased Mary's attention span. A
chiropractor was consulted and adjustment aided in relieving the
swelling and pressure on the brain. With regular treatment, Mary's head
plates began to hold a normal position enabling her body to receive
complete information though the senses and store knowledge gained in
the brain.

Mary now talks easily with her brothers and sisters, and any
adults willing to keep up with her energetic pace. Now when she has
difficulty communicating her ideas and thoughts she says, "I can't say
that" instead of throwing a temper tantrum. This opens the door to
greater learning.

Health Analyses reveal the parents' role in rearing a child.
Suggestions are often given to the parents to aid them in being a healthy
influence during the child's formulative years. The parental role is
indeed a catalyst for the learning and viewpoints a child will experience
as he grows older. The following readings were requested by a mother
of two sons, ages six months and eighteen months. This analysis reveals
that both sons are a reflection of those in their environment. The
information in each analysis gave the parents suggestions for mental,

emotional, and physical improvement. This first excerpt was for John, the eighteen-month-old.

> *"We see a scattering of attention. We see that this one is in need of being able to build the will and focus this one's attention on one singular thing at a time. We see that this one is being bombarded by experiences and does not quickly catalogue them or store them as memory. We see as a result, much of this one's existence is emotional, and we see that this one reacts to the environment readily.*
>
> *We see that this one, most of the time mirrors whatever is being exhibited around him. We see that there is a need for fashioning the identity of this one, there is a need for stimulating the senses individually rather than collectively. This would aid this one in being able to collect information and store it.*
>
> *We see within the physical body that the major disruption is within the digestive tract. There is a type of reaction that occurs in the stomach area which is similar to that of defenselessness emotionally. We do not find there is an actual physical disorder. There is too much acid at these times released too early that then mixes with food producing a plethora of acid causing upset. Would suggest this one be calm at the time of eating and the environment be calm."*

Further evidence of the environmental influence and the parental role affecting the child is revealed when the parent asks why the child almost always wakes crying and cranky.

> *"We see that this one is not in a bad mood when this occurs. We see that this is the only way this one knows of gaining the attention, and this is mental attention as well as physical attention. This is not an indication that something is wrong, it is the only means this one has at the present time to get what this one wants."*

The parent was also concerned about the child whining

throughout the day for long periods of time. The analysis indicated there was nothing physically wrong with this child, rather the child had learned to whine for a specific purpose. The parents were inconsistent in giving the child attention, and the reading revealed why he was developing the habit of whining.

> *"This is learned behavior. We see that it is this one's way of getting attention. This one is learning how to use it in this way." (7-11-89-11-BGO)*

Both John's and Bradley's (the six-month-old son) analyses revealed similarities concerning environmental influences and the need for the parents to teach these children how to focus their attention and build concentration skills. Even at six months, Bradley's reading revealed how he is beginning to imagine himself as a failure.

> *"We see for this one's mind to race. We see for this one to be able to take in information and want to do something with it very quickly. We see that many of the things this one does with it are not the result of a concentrated effort; therefore, this one fails often. We see that this one is beginning to build a pattern of thinking of the Self as a failure and we see that much of this has been encouraged by the environment. We see this one to find it difficult to be able to explain the Self and this is causing this one some disruption as well. Would suggest that this one learn to hold the attention for a period of time upon one thing. Would suggest that this one be stimulated to sharpen the memory and be encouraged to use the imagination. In this way this one would be able to use the skills to think more completely. We see this one is ready to reason, but is short on the skills for this to occur. This one has much motivation and this one has much drive, and it is from these things that the energy comes forth. It is up to this one to channel the energy, to direct it in ways that would be profitable to the Self." (7-11-89-12-BGO)*

When a child reaches the age of seven, although still guided by his parents' patterns and influences, he is on his way to being an individual. At this age, the reasoning skills have sufficiently developed and the child begins to separate productive experiences from those which are not productive.

An analysis was requested by a mother of an eighteen-year-old who was suffering from nightly seizures. As a student of metaphysics, the mother speculated about the mental cause of this disorder, wondering if the physical condition could be treated wholistically. The mother was also concerned that her daughter might have a brain tumor or dysfunction of the brain. The analysis revealed that the seizures were physically produced by a build-up of too many toxins in the bloodstream that settled in the head area. This was mentally caused by a repression of the woman's desires for self-expression from fears of not being accepted by others. The reading gave suggestions for determining a spiritual life path which would increase the capacity to receive ideas from others. Physical suggestions included additional iron, magnesium, and potassium, as well as spinal alignment.

Having this information, the Conductor pursued more information concerning how the woman could better express herself on a daily basis. This led to inquiries concerning how she could determine a career which would be an aid to her health rather than a detriment. These types of questions whether initiated by the person receiving the reading or by the Conductor aid in understanding and putting into use the information gained in Health Analyses.

Karmic Lessons to Learn

There are individuals who receive Health Analyses who are not experiencing illness. Rather, these people are curious about what information will be given in a mental, emotional, and physical analysis. Since we exist as physical beings for the purpose of learning, each of us have areas where changes could bring improvement. Many times we wait until we experience discomfort or disease before attempting to find why a condition exists in our lives. By understanding cause, we can insure a cure. Health or disease begins within our thinking. The physical existence is the place where we are able to build understandings and mastery. The physical world was created to serve us in our quest for learning. The perspective offered by a Health Reading can aid us in accelerating that learning, making our lives more fulfilling.

Have you ever seen someone who is mentally retarded or someone with a physical deformity and wondered why God would have created such sorrow? I have, and in my search for truth have found that everything has a purpose. Congenital disorders are sometimes threatening and frightening. Yet from the soul's perspective, there is much that can be gained from this experience. Health Analyses have revealed this many times. I have always been curious about why some people would experience mental retardation or physical disability. My curiosity led to a desire to aid these individuals which in turn led to my pursuit of a Recreational Therapist degree. While researching thousands of transcripts of readings, one stood out. This was a man born with cerebral palsy. Amazingly, the reading stated very few difficulties in the mental and emotional systems. Difficulties in transferring the messages from the senses to the brain and in the nervous system being able to send transmissions from the brain to the physical system were noted. Learning how to visualize the brain and nervous system working properly was one of the recommendations for this man. The analysis suggested in order to do this, the man would need to learn to hold an image in the mind very strongly until this image could be transferred to the brain cells through the nerves enabling information to be relayed in a steady flow of electrical current.

Since this condition was from birth, the man asked why this type of body was chosen. The response was enlightening for it centered in the individual's potential learning. The reading emphasized how attempting to correct the physical difficulties rather than just allowing them to remain in the current, limited condition, would build understandings in the Self thus fulfilling karmic obligations.

What a new revelation this becomes! The soul or subconscious mind is like a puzzle which reflects the blueprint of our maturity to be Thinkers. The soul holds the understandings we have gained. Each understanding is one piece in the puzzle of our whole Self. To insure our continued evolution, the Universal Law of Cause and Effect operates in our lives as what is commonly referred to as karma. To understand what our karmic obligations are and to add understanding to our Selves causes all the pieces of our puzzles to fit together becoming whole and complete. A soul can choose the condition of a body to learn something very important to its evolution.

Not long ago, there was an innovative study of children with leukemia. Research doctors had the children visualize their red blood cells as soldiers fighting the "enemy" white blood cells. After a period of time, the experimenters discovered this play therapy of visualization aided in the healing of these children. Many people who receive Health Analyses share this type of innovative approach to wholistic health. One young woman, through her belief in the power of her mind and through her efforts is able to walk after being paralyzed for five years. Another woman, following the removal of a cancerous breast, used the suggestions in Health Readings to change destructive thinking patterns, healing her body of cancer without the assistance of chemotherapy and radiation treatments. What hope and respect can be produced in the mind of mankind when he realizes that through holding healthy thoughts firmly in mind the condition of the physical body can be altered. We can begin to see that the condition of the physical body can be changed when we learn the secrets of healing.

Years ago I was curious in a more common way. I was facing a major change in my life, preparing to move from my hometown in Chicago. I was also attached to my fears, stubbornly holding onto them. During a Health Analysis, I intended to ask questions that might assist me in this making this transition easier, and found the body of the reading addressed my conflict.

"We see that there have been some changes that have occurred in regards to this one's own image of the self, but there has not been the consistency of holding onto this or working in a way which will cause the results according to this one's desires. Would suggest that there is much strength that this one does not utilize in a way which would cause forward motion and that because of the rigidity spoken of there is the tendency for this one to place attention on the inabilities of the self rather than the abilities of the self. We see that as this one begins the process of imagining changes for herself this one uses that of rigidity as a way to do this, therefore creating impossible ideas for her own self to fulfill. Would suggest that this one create a more fluid movement of

the self that this is not seen as a type of passivity but as perpetual motion. This will be accomplished if this one will begin to initiate internal changes as well as external changes and to follow through upon them rather than being so sporadic. We see that in regards to the abilities of the self to gain a sense of confidence or trust there is the tendency once again to hold to the rigidity rather than to begin the process of experimentation on a consistent basis. This one places a great deal of attention on that of fear and that of anger. Would suggest to this one that as this one begins to utilize the imagination in a more constructive manner, this one will cease to need to become so angry and so put out by herself."
(7-15-81-6-GBM)

This information gave me great insights into my Self. I had been toying with the idea of moving out of Chicago where I had lived all of my twenty-six years. Surrounded by people who had known me all my life, it had become very difficult to make changes in my expression and how I was received by others. The image that kept coming to me was of a seed which had all the possibilities and capabilities of being a strong plant, however the soil where it was planted was filled with insects waiting to destroy its growth. I don't think any of my loved ones were aware of their influence in my life, and I didn't think they were insects, but I desired a change and was beginning to realize that it was time to leave the nest.

Shortly after receiving this analysis, I moved to Tulsa some 700 miles from my hometown. I used the strength within me to overcome the common fears of loneliness, rejection, and failure. I remembered times when I would change jobs and be able to make friends quickly. With this in mind, I made friends in my new home. I also kept holy the image of who I wanted to become and began to practice being that strong, confident, and loving person. I knew no one in Tulsa was aware of the old me, therefore, the soil was fresh and fertile for my seed ideas to grow. By making this one decision to move, I learned the freedom you can have when you use your imagination.

A Second Opinion

Many individuals over the past years have used the readings as a second opinion, especially when faced with the possibility of surgery. Those diagnosed with life threatening diseases such as cancer or AIDS have used readings to determine if the treatment medically suggested is the best treatment to use. These individuals also seek the information a reading provides concerning how they can create new and different attitudes that will produce health in the body.

Having a degree in Recreational Therapy and being in the health field, I know it is a common practice for doctors to suggest to patients who are facing major health decisions to seek a second opinion. More and more professionals in the health field are considering the information in these readings as such a resource. I believe as more and more physicians become aware of the information and completeness of the Health Analysis, they too will use this resource to assist in caring for those who desire wholeness and health. I imagine in the near future, health professionals will be using these readings as a way of obtaining valuable insight to make their careers more effective for patients and more fulfilling for themselves. I have seen progress taking place in the medical field for many years. Doctors are beginning to accept the influence a person's attitude and thoughts have on the health of the physical body. Most doctors accept the basic truth that stress causes pressure and dis-ease in the body, even when they do not understand why this is so.

One afternoon I was in the office of the School of Metaphysics center in Berwyn, a suburb of Chicago. I received a call from a woman who had heard me on the radio. The subject of the interview included how nonproductive mental attitudes can cause physical disorders and diseases, and how someone could change these thoughts to ones causing forward motion in life thus healing the physical disorder. This woman had a vested interest in calling as she asked, "Do you think you can teach me how to heal myself so I can walk again?"

I paused for a moment, considering the depth of what she was asking. I first suggested she receive a Health Reading because I knew it would give both of us information we could use. I also knew the Health Readings were complete, truthful and objective, and her reading would let both of us know if this was possible. We discussed how to secure an appointment, and we both awaited the day of the readings.

Joann arrived at the School driving her own car, but she needed help getting her wheelchair from the trunk of the car, and she needed help being carried up the stairs. She, along with others who were receiving readings, sat around the living room waiting for her turn.

I learned Joann had bruised her spine in a diving accident at the age of fifteen about three years before receiving this reading. She had been told by most of her doctors that she would probably never walk again. To her surprise, the reading reported that physically she could regain the ability to walk.

> *"We see that in the mental system there has been for a very long period of time desire upon this one's part to have a sense of importance in regards to the self and in regards to a sense of productivity and creativity. We see that there has not however been the action taken upon this one's part to produce in a way that would bring about a sense of importance for her own self. We see therefore there has been a tendency for this one to avoid taking the responsibility for the development of this one's own sense of identity and the responsibility for taking the control of this one's own power.*
>
> *We see that there is much indecision being experienced at the present time and a tendency for this one to hesitate in moving forward or putting out effort in a way that would produce exact results that are desired by the self. Would suggest that this one cease removing the self as being a cause in this one's circumstances and situations and begin seeing how this one's thoughts do produce the resultant facts.*
>
> *We see that this one has wanted to remove the self from specific circumstances and conditions that this one has experienced discomfort and lack of confidence in. We see that this one has lost sight of purpose for achieving upon the part of the inner self as well as the external self, therefore, there have been conditions in which this one has been forced to establish a sense of priority and a sense of perspective that will cause action by this one. We see however that there is also hesitancy*

in regards to this. Would suggest to this one that as long as the hesitation continues there will continue to be placed before the self situations which will produce forced change."

Joann's learning was to make decisions and act on them. She had practiced looking for her importance outside of herself for seventeen years. When life didn't seem to give her a fair deal, she would play the role of the victim. Even though Joann was not at all pleased with herself, her hesitation in refusing to regain her ability to walk centered on her lack of purpose rather than physical disability. The Conductor of her reading asked why Joann was able to tense and relax muscles in her legs while under hypnosis but not at other times.

"There was not a true desire for effects at this time because of the lack of purpose as has been related. We see a positive effect (due to) the recognition on a subtle degree that there is the possibility of movement. We see however that this has not been brought into this one's conscious working awareness, therefore there is the tendency for this one to hang onto what cannot be rather than what can be. We see therefore this one relies upon states of mind that are not conducive to bringing about actual change. Would suggest that it will be through this one's development of that which would be called will, conscious will, which will produce the results. This will be done in a way which this one gains control in a concentrated manner." (5-31-81-7-GBM)

Joann was happy to hear that she might be able to walk again. With this goal in mind, Joann started learning how to heal her body by taking classes in applied metaphysics. She was in for the challenge of her life, because she needed to become honest in the ways she used and misused others in her life. I had the honor of teaching Joann when she began her studies. As a recreational therapist, I had met patients who were more physically limited so Joann could not play on my emotions as easily as she had done with others. This was her first obstacle to overcome, because now she had to pull her own weight.

I taught Joann how to set goals for herself on a weekly basis that would move her closer to accomplishing her desire to walk. They included many activities we take for granted: bathing without assistance, climbing up and down staircases by using her arms and buttocks, and having her wheelchair placed behind her driver's seat so Joann could reach it without assistance. Joann faced herself with each step she took. She saw how she misused others to be in control. She could also see how determined and purposeful she could be.

One situation is still very clear in my mind as the turning point for Joann. She had come to class late, angry when I addressed her disrespectful tardiness. Feeding her anger was my refusal to assist her in moving her wheelchair over a curb. The entire class period, Joann found more situations to add to her anger. At the end of class I asked another student to assist in taking Joann downstairs. He obliged, even helping her into her car. I went to hug Joann goodbye, looked her straight in the eyes and told her she would never walk again because it was so easy for her to let others do what she already knew how to do.

The next week Joann was ready to face herself. She wanted to understand and use the suggestions in her analysis and was ready to cause there to be purpose in her actions. Now she was open to changing her way of thinking and her progress was accelerated.

Another example of someone who used a Health Analysis for a second opinion of her condition was a friend of mine living in Memphis, Tennessee. A health conscious individual, Mary began feeling fatigued and out of sorts for no apparent reason. When this persisted for days and grew worse, she decided to go to an outpatient clinic for diagnosis. By the time she arrived at the hospital, her fever was 103 degrees. After waiting to see someone for several hours, she was examined by a doctor who told her she had appendicitis and recommended she be admitted into the hospital immediately to have her appendix removed.

Mary was shocked at the idea of even considering an operation, told the doctor she was going to get a Health Analysis, got dressed and left. Mary had had repeated experiences with Health Analyses both personally and as a long time teacher of metaphysics. She knew if her condition was the result of difficulties in the appendix a Health Analysis would confirm it, and if her difficulty was something else she would also discover this in a Health Analysis.

Having arranged for the reading through SOM headquarters,

Mary also made arrangements to speak with the Conductor following her reading so she could receive the information as soon as possible. When Mary called, Dr. Jerry Rothermel, the Conductor of her reading, reported that the analysis spoke of inflammation and infection in the abdominal area, particularly the colon, but did not indicate disease in the appendix or any need for surgery. He suggested she see another doctor for symptomatic relief of the infection.

Upon visiting another hospital and another doctor, Mary discovered her infection and pain were the result not of her appendix but of a brown recluse spider bite. Since Mary was a student of metaphysics, she was aware that her way of thinking had produced this near-death experience. She had been punishing herself. All of her life she had experienced periods of depression, not knowing why. These constant bouts stimulated her search for truth. She was also acquainted with self-defeating attitudes, but not yet aware of how to change them in herself. The analysis gave Mary a clear description of her troubling thoughts and suggestions for resolving them. She listened to the mental and emotional parts of her analysis very carefully.

> *"We see confusion in the mental system, and we see this has arisen because there is a large amount of pain that this one is experiencing mentally, emotionally, and physically. We see for this one to entertain thoughts that this is this one's punishment for past thoughts and actions that are less than this one feels they should be.*
>
> *This one is in need of being able to move the self forward, and to be able to achieve a state of calmness so that this one can begin to use memory more accurately. We see that at these times this one cuts off the use of imagination and dwells upon the past and upon what should have been. Would suggest to this one to use concentration to clear the thinking. Would suggest that this one place within the mind this one's imagined goals rather than to dwell upon the past in the way that has been described. Would suggest that then this one could begin to use the creativity to move towards what this one wants, rather than to destroy it." (7-11-89-9-BGO)*

This Health Analysis saved Mary from further pain, unnecessary surgery, and medical bills. The medical profession is important and with the information in this analysis coupled with antibiotics she received from the doctor, Mary was able to speed her recovery. Knowing the accuracy of medical diagnosis is also important for both the patient and the physician. Using a Health Analysis as a resource as Mary did, can accelerate diagnosis, treatment and recovery to health.

Sometimes physical conditions have been accurately diagnosed by medical professionals. These diagnoses produce many questions in the mind of the patient that can be answered in a Health Analysis. Many times people ask about medications, wanting to know if they are necessary for the body, if they are harmful, and if there are more natural ways to cause healing. One individual who was taking the drug Dilantin wanted to know if there were any side effects or nonproductive effects from the use of this drug. The reading revealed the following:

> *"We see that there is some difficulty that does occur in the liver in terms of toxins which this body has difficulty releasing. We see that this does help to create a balance in this one's electrical system, but we see that the primary difficulty in taking this drug is that it keeps this one's attention removed from the cause for the difficulty – this one's having accepted failure within the Self, having accepted that this one will not be able to fulfill this one's desire, and the subsequent anger that is built within self. Would suggest that this one work with some form of doctor or counselor if this one would desire to eliminate this drug, and that this not be removed all at once. By this one learning how to change the mental and emotional attitudes, this one could get to a place where this would not be necessary."* (7-2-91-4-LJF)

This man asked about a grand mal seizure he had recently experienced and the reading revealed this was caused by the build-up of anger noted in the excerpt above. Since the drug Dilantin was used to prevent such seizures, the man now had knowledge of how he could learn to use and express his anger and working with his doctor move toward a life free from the use of chemicals.

In most cases Health Analyses are given only with the consent of the individual receiving the reading. In this way respect is maintained for an individual and his desires. When someone is unconscious or unable to make this type of decision for himself, a family member or guardian may request the analysis.

Analyses can aid family members and loved ones as well as the person receiving the reading. In the following case, a Health Analysis was requested by a man whose father was hospitalized for cancer treatment. The father was receiving chemotherapy and his doctors wanted to begin experimental treatments with a new liquid chemical. This treatment was seen by professionals as a final attempt to treat a terminally ill patient. The son wanted to know if this treatment was beneficial or detrimental. He also wanted to know if his father wanted to continue to live because he wanted to aid his father on whatever path he chose. The reading highlighted a need for the father to recognize that although there were counteractive measures taking place within his body for healing, he needed to cooperate with those efforts. This would be accomplished by accepting his value and sharing with others what he had learned through his life. The reader emphasized it is not the body that determines the time of death or becomes diseased on its own, rather the individual's thinking and the goals determine the capability of producing health or disease within the body.

To aid this man in being able to heal himself and cause the changes needed, the Conductor of the reading asked for the mental cause for the man's cancer and why it had manifested in the lymphatic system. The mental cause was identified as apathy with emotional reactions of hurt and disappointment that there had not been something more to the life. The man was described as being oblivious to what he had accomplished through his lifetime. Suggestions included to recognize the lives he had touched, what he had learned, and to be more open and intentional about giving to people what he wanted to give to them. These attitudes would not be conducive to the production of cancer within the liver. It was noted that the lymphatic cancer was secondary to the cancer in the liver.

For the cancer to be healed, this man needed to create a more positive attitude and greater will for life. There were certain side effects that would come as a result of the new treatment because of his attitudes. The treatment alone could not cause life, only the man's own attitudes could do this. The changes in mental attitude along with the treatments would cause a healing condition in the body.

With this information, the son accepted that it would be his father's choice to either cause healing or to withdraw from the physical. This aided the son in being able to see there was a reason for this condition and that the control was in his father's hands. When the Conductor asked for further suggestions for the family members, it was noted that when they gave attention to the body only, they did themselves a disservice and did not open up their minds to receive what the man had to give to them. It was suggested they overcome fears of being hurt and open their own thinking to receive whatever the man might have to say to them. The importance to their own learning of how they responded was addressed.

Modern medicine does have its place, but so often man looks for a miracle drug that will take away the pain without attempting to make internal changes in his thoughts and attitudes. The mind is a very powerful tool that has the capability of causing health as well as disease. The Health Analysis can be used in many ways to aid you to be in touch with your true Self. They provide honest information giving you the control to make a difference in your state of health.

Hope

Throughout the ages, man has created a variety of diseases and disorders. When these arise, man searches for an antidote to stop their destructive effects on society. During the time of Jesus of Nazareth, leprosy was common, killing thousands people in the Middle East. In the 1950's polio spread through America, crippling and killing many. In the last three decades, cancer has been the disease frightening society. Even with scientific treatments to retard cancer cell growth, cancer remains a major cause of physical death. In the late 80's and 90's AIDS continues to spread world-wide reaching epidemic proportions.

I have chosen to dedicate this section to those who have had such diseases and have recovered. I only hope I can stimulate you to see that there is a cure for all diseases. Through using information and insight gained in a Health Analysis, you can learn the kinds of thinking that need to be changed to cause such healing.

This is a story about a woman named Joyce. Joyce, a student in metaphysics, thought no harm could come upon her life. Joyce had been with her daughter who had just given birth to a daughter. This was quite a joyous occasion. Her daughter's doctor had walked in to see how everything was going, took one look at Joyce and knew something was wrong. He instructed her to see him the next day. With this visit, Joyce was diagnosed with breast cancer.

Several months before this diagnosis, Joyce had received a Health Analysis. She had noticed a lump in her breast and inquired about it. The reading had noted a cessation of motion in several glands resulting in a collection of tissue. The analysis said although there was no malignancy present, there was potential for it because she harbored long-standing resentments. Specific suggestions were given for releasing the past by giving her Self something to look foward to in the present and future.

Joyce, a gregarious person outwardly, realized she had not heeded this message. She had failed to change her ways of thinking, continuing to hold the resentment noted in her reading, and now the collection of tissue in her breast had developed into a malignant tumor. Joyce consented to undergo an operation to remove the tumor and her breast. With new resolve, she actively sought ways to change her attitudes and subsequent lifestyle. She began the healing process and was released from the hospital shortly after her operation.

She was asked and encouraged by her doctor to undergo chemotherapy. Knowing many of the ill effects of this kind of treatment, Joyce requested a Health Analysis to gain perspective before making this decision.

> *"We see ideas of victimization in the mental system. These have been produced over a long period of time and are part of a type of self degradation and irresponsibility that this one has built. We see that this one has put the self in abusive situations in the past and has built much animosity and resentment toward that. However, much of this is directed outwardly rather than this one accepting responsibility for how this one has created her own ways of thinking and her own emotions. We see that this one is battling the self in*

terms of who has control of the self, whether it is other people
as this one sees it or herself. We see, in reality, this one is
battling the self. It has nothing to do with other people. It
is this one's attempt to force control of the self without the
understanding of this. We see this is stealing needed energy
from the mental, emotional, and physical systems at the
present time. Would suggest that rather than be fear
motivated, as this one is, that it would be of greater benefit
for this one to learn how to calm and relax the mind,
mentally, emotionally, and physically in order for this one to
be able to create the state of mind this one would need in
order to direct the attention in a more profitable way."

Faced with the possibilities of having any further cancer sites,
Joyce struggled to remember when she first experienced unworthiness
and self-degradation. Joyce's trip down memory lane took her to
thoughts of her father and the relationship she had with him. She told
of a story when she was around six years old. Her father, an executive
for Standard Oil, often travelled but this day was home. Joyce remembered sitting on the floor, playing with the Sunday newspaper, pretending to read. Her father was nearby.   Seeing that she held the stock
section he was looking for, he reached down and took the page from her
hands. Joyce remembered thinking, "What? I was reading that! How
can he just do that?" Instead of saying something, Joyce formed her own
conclusion that she did not count for much.

From this beginning, she continued to add to this thought form
as she grew older until finally the cells of her body began to stagnate
from the repeated "I can't" attitudes. Through adult years, her thoughts
had grown to include "others have but I don't deserve" and "I desire but
I don't have what it takes". This was the false way of thinking cited in
her analysis. Joyce's desire to change was also addressed in the
suggestions offered for productive thinking.

In this same reading, Joyce asked if there were any sites of
cancer remaining in her body.

"We do not find malignancy at this time, although there are
areas of susceptibility. One being the one that was given in
the area of the colon. There are some sites of what could be

skin cancer. There is some difficulty in the area of the thyroid that would lean toward this as well. Also the liver."
(7-12-88-12-GBM)

Asking if chemotherapy would be beneficial, Joyce discovered it would affect the susceptible areas but would be detrimental to the body as a whole. Since she knew that for permanent healing to occur she would need to change the attitudes described, she asked how she could have more loving thoughts. The reading gave this insight.

"This would first be in the relaxation spoken of, then the practice of concentration so this one can direct and control the thinking. These would be the first steps that this one would practice." (7-12-88-12-GBM)

With these insights, Joyce began gathering information from all quarters of the world: the American Cancer Society, nutritionists and food specialists, holistic health centers, and alternative treatments. She started giving care and attention to her thoughts and attitudes, pursuing spiritual disciplines with more devotion and purpose.

Several turning points occurred aiding Joyce to make the decision to begin healing herself from within. She discovered there were several people who wanted to aid her in her search for health and life. She studied her analysis with her teacher, Dr. Daniel Condron, and with a friend Lucy Galarza, a registered nurse. Examining the reading word-for-word helped Joyce discover her first thoughts of hate and self-destruction. After an intense session with her teacher, Joyce requested mental healing projections be performed to assist her recovery. The night of the first projection, she knew that a large portion of the cancer had disappeared. She also knew that her course of action must be one in which she could have full faith and trust. She knew all other treatments could do something for her, such as chemotherapy, radiation, or healing spas, but the key for Joyce was her faith, belief and willingness to change.

Joyce put her complete confidence in her ability to heal herself and opened herself to aid from others. She received monthly Health Analyses from the School of Metaphysics to monitor her progress and stimulate steps for further recovery. She began to notice changes happening quickly. Her skin improved, the light returned to her eyes, and she experienced an increase in energy. Her health was being restored. Just six months after surgery, she moved from Madison, Wisconsin, to Kenosha. When helpers were unavailable, Joyce proved to herself that her health was back by making the move unassisted.

Joyce continued to receive Health Analyses until her desired conclusion was verified. By the end of June, 1989, her greatest hope was affirmed when the reader saw no evidence of cancer anywhere in the body. Just six months after being diagnosed with terminal cancer, Joyce was completely cancer free. A karmic obligation initiated in 1936 was now relieved in 1989. Joyce continues to experience life fully, and she will tell you she is healthier now than she was five years ago!

There have been others like Joyce who have used Health Analyses to communicate the progress they are making. Many use readings as a teaching tool for health, receiving them frequently as feedback. An objective source can offer information and insight to accelerate the manifestation of our goals. For this reason, many receive yearly "check-ups" for the timely evaluations of attitudes and emotional states offered in Health Analyses. Others request an analysis when a physical problem occurs.

Whenever there is a disorder or disease in the body, its point of origin is a way of thinking which is disrespectful to the Self. Over time, when these thoughts remain unexpressed a dysfunction occurs. Thoughts are things. The way you think, what you think, the care you take in your thinking, affects you and the world around you. It is often uncomfortable for people to realize and admit they are responsible for their circumstances and conditions.

Through our experiences on this earthly plane, we gain the understanding of our origin and our purpose for existence. Too often we become distracted by our sense pleasures believing these are our reason for existence. In times of loss or disorder, we are forced to bring our attention back to the whole point of our lives which is to learn so we may gain the understandings for compatibility with our Creator. Man can learn a great deal from his body if he will only take time to listen. There is always a mental cause, a lack or error in thinking, which over time will seek to express itself causing disorder or disease in the physical body.

By understanding cause, we can then cause healing.

Health and disease start in the thinking. The state of your health can communicate to you something more–it can tell you the health of your thoughts. The physical is the place to serve us in adding to our learning and maturing as souls. A Health Analysis can assist you in your quest for soul progression as well as wholeness and well-being.

Sheila Benjamin received a Bachelor of Science degree in Recreation Therapy from Southern Illinois Unversity in Carbondale in 1978. Having studied and taught applied metaphysics for over fifteen years, Sheila has combined her traditional educational background with the progressive ideas and skills she has learned in the School of Metaphysics to enhance her effectiveness as a therapist. To broaden her understanding of wholistic health, she pursued and received certification as a Psi Counselor. Sheila received a Doctorate of Divinity degree in 1992, enabling her to minister to the spiritual needs of the many people she meets.

Dedicated to enriching the lives of others, Dr. Sheila is one of the individuals who has received training as a Reader. She earned her Doctorate in Metaphysics in 1994, and often hosts Spiritual Initiation Sessions at Moon Valley Ranch on the College of Metaphysics campus. She and her husband Brad make their home in Tulsa, Oklahoma.

*"A man is known
by the company he organizes."*
Ambrose Bierce (1881)

Business Analyses
by Laurel Jan Clark, B.A., D.M.

A Business Has a Mind of its Own

As young children, most of us formulate ideas of what we want to be when we grow up. Inherent in the idea of what we want to become is an awareness that we each are unique and have some talent or gift to offer to humanity. As children, we are blessed with the idealism to believe we can have what we want, to be who we want to be, and to follow a calling which will provide a vehicle for us to serve others. We think of a vocation as a means for self expression, a place to create and fulfill our desires.

Most children have vivid imaginations and believe anything is possible. Stimulated by stories, television, and fantasy games, a child may decide to be a superhero, bringing order into a world of chaos or conquering evil villains. He could imagine becoming a nurse or doctor, healing pain and disease. She might want to be a lawyer, to champion justice and right the world's wrongs. They could picture themselves as singers or dancers, inspiring people with beauty, grace, and power. In their games and fantasies, children pretend to be adults. They imagine themselves giving to the world. We all do this at some time in our lives, but when we are very young we listen closely to our innermost Self. We have contact with the pure essence of ourselves, our soul's desire. As we grow older, we tend to listen more to outside influences and think about what we "should" do, what fits in with others' expectations, rather than what we want.

In considering the idea of what we want to be, we are in touch with an assignment for this lifetime. We give ourselves an assignment for each lifetime, based on understandings we have already built and understandings we want to build. You could call this your heart's desire. Some people relate to this idea as their purpose for existence. If you think of yourself as a soul using a physical body and physical experiences for learning, life becomes a schoolroom. Similar to completing grades in grammar school or high school, we complete lessons in life to progress up the ladder of soul evolution. A young child thinks with this perspective of who they are and who they want to become and thus imagines the mission they want to fulfill.

As we grow older, many of us are taught to accept the idea that we are physical (not spiritual) beings and that life is a struggle for physical survival. The idea of a calling or vocation can become distorted so that we think of a career only as a means to make money to provide food, clothing, and shelter for our physical bodies. We learn to forget what we want to <u>be</u> and focus instead on what we want to <u>do</u>. When this happens, we make choices based on how lucrative a job will be even if it is not personally satisfying. While it is important to make money, "Man does not live on bread alone, but on every word that comes from the mouth of God" (Matthew 4:4).

If our attention becomes engrossed in satisfying physical desires, it is easy to forget to feed our souls. We forget that life is a schoolroom, a place to use experiences to create who we are. Instead, life becomes a chore. We create incessant physical desires and become slaves to our desires – for the more physical things we want, the more money we require, and the more we lust for the things we don't have. This type of existence provides fleeting comfort without any lasting satisfaction.

To reawaken the idea of our true nature as a soul or a spiritual being means considering the question, "Who am I?" When we choose a profession as a vehicle to create our identity, we can once again enjoy life. We find contentment in giving of ourselves. We can put our physical desires into proper perspective, for if we are satisfying our soul's needs, the hunger to accumulate physical possessions lessens. The work we do then becomes a joy, for when we are creating we love what we do.

Imagine what a different world it would be if everyone used his or her job as a place to give, to create, to use and develop talents and skills, to fulfill ideals! People would enjoy going to work and daily living would provide peace and contentment.

In search of contentment and job satisfaction, people often create businesses of their own. Unfortunately, they don't always find spiritual and material abundance. To aid business people to create productive and meaningful careers, the School of Metaphysics developed Business Analyses. A business owner or manager can use a Business Analysis to discover how to make their vocation a vehicle for self-expression, for themselves and their employees. They can learn how to increase profits, to hire people whose ideals are compatible with their own, to expand sales, to eliminate areas of waste, to uncover hidden resources, to identify key markets; in fact, to improve every aspect of the company.

Creating a business is like giving birth to and raising a child. The business has an identity of its own. The owner or manager directs and guides its growth, nurtures it, responds to its needs, and heals it when necessary. We call the owner or manager the "directing intelligence." To direct means "to regulate the activities or course of; to carry out the organizing, energizing and supervising of; to determine the course of." Intelligence is "the ability to learn or understand; the ability to apply knowledge to manipulate one's environment." The "directing intelligence", therefore, is the one who gives direction to the business and whose judgment determines its efficacy. His or her thinking influences the business, and any difficulties within the company can be cured by identifying and changing the way of thinking which is causing the problem.

The Business Analysis is similar to a Health Reading, relating the mental, emotional, and physical disorders in a company with suggestions for correcting any disorders. "Health" refers to a state of being sound, or whole. When we talk about the "health" of a business, we are referring to its condition, and what is needed to cause it to function well. A business has a mind, which is the collective attitude of all the individuals who are a part of its makeup. It has emotion, which is the collective emotions of all those who are involved with the business. And it has a body, the structure or vehicle which is comprised of the people, places, and things which form the business enterprise. The Business Analyses address all elements of a business, for if there is any one part that isn't functioning properly, the whole business will be influenced.

Business Analyses, like Health Readings, are designed to pinpoint the areas of dis-order and to remove them. They identify <u>causes</u> for problems, and therein lies the real value, for permanent solutions may be found by addressing and changing the cause. Other types of business analyses will deal with symptoms, but applying "band-aid" solutions to correct the effects of disordered thinking only lasts for awhile. If you view a business as a living organism, a change in one area will affect every other area. A "diseased" part will sap the energy from the healthy parts, so merely changing one problem area without changing its cause only temporarily corrects the problem.

Business Analyses are done from the third level of consciousness where all thoughts begin to form. We have found that everything begins with thought. The universal law of cause and effect states that thought is cause, and effect is its manifest likeness. This law applies to the formation of any object in all Creation, including the formation of a business.

If this is a difficult concept to grasp, examine the chair in which you are sitting as you read this book. Someone designed the image or blueprint of this chair in his or her mind before it could be formed into a physical object. Look at your face in the mirror some day when you have accomplished a goal. You will see the beauty, joy, and confidence reflected in your features. Then look in the mirror on a day when you are angry or disappointed. You will find your physical features unattractive and unpleasant. Or try this experiment to discover the power of thought: use two plants and take care of them with the same amount of water, food, and sunlight. Touch one plant lovingly every day, and say to it with affection, "I love you. You are beautiful." Look at the other plant every day and say to it, "I hate you. I wish you would die." Be sincere and mean what you say in both cases. You will find that your love will cause the first plant to flourish and your hatred will cause the second plant to wither.

Many people are taught to believe that their thoughts aren't real. Do you remember as a child, having an idea you thought was great, and someone told you, "Oh, you're so idealistic, that will never happen!" When we learn to believe these limitations, we learn to accept the lie that our thoughts have no reality. In fact, our thoughts cause our lives, our world, and our existence.

The thoughts, then, of the directing intelligence of the company, are important to the functioning of the business as a whole. The directing intelligence leads everyone else who is involved with his or her business and his sphere of influence is the company. While the directing intelligence is not the only person involved in a company's success or failure, his or her thoughts set the pace and guide the formation of the company.

For example, a children's clothing designer/distributor in Anchorage, Alaska was experiencing difficulties because the owner had become distracted from her original ideals:

> *"We see a scattering of energies within this business. We see that there is difficulty in terms of the intelligent direction having a sense of comfort and control of the activities. We see that there is a kind of insecurity that does arise and therefore this does then concern others within the business as to what decisions should be made at certain times. We see that this is not what was expected upon the part of the directing intelligence for we see that there were many creative ideas that this one held and we see that there was an awareness of need for this particular company but in developing it, it has somewhat moved away from this one's dream and we see that there is frustration experienced upon that one's part and a great deal of worry."*

As a result, the entire company was affected:

> *"We see that many times there is such a fluctuation of the business workings itself, the scattering of energies become very pronounced upon everyone's part and we see that at those times there is over concern and worry that does exist in terms of the quality of the products being produced and put out and the ability to meet orders."*

The Business Analysis highlighted the importance of the directing intelligence as a catalyst for change:

> *"In order for this business to move and to prosper there needs to be someone who will be the driving force of this operation." (5-28-91-4-BGO)*

For success in any business a positive mental attitude is a requirement, not just an asset. The following analysis on a small business opened in this way:

> *"We see within the mental system there is a desire for success. We do see along with this desire for success that there is also a kind of fear that this will not come about. We see therefore there is some difficulty in being able to cause there to be motion mentally within this business. Would suggest there be formulated a very clear, distinct, and detailed plan. Would suggest that this start with the directing intelligence formulating a clear ideal first in regards to this one personally, then including the individuals this one wants to serve."*

As the reading continued, specific instruction in the steps for creating a successful and profitable company were given. Of particular import to the woman receiving the reading, the way the information was related gives insight that is universally applicable for anyone beginning a new business or reorganizing an existing one.

> *"Would suggest this be a very idealistic goal in terms of this one incorporating the highest aspirations, highest ideals, and the very highest that this one can imagine for and from the self. We see that it was originally this highest aspiration that did stimulate this one to even want to create a business in the first place.*
>
> *Before this one adds to this any type of specific physical plans of action, this one needs to include what will be offered to other individuals....the qualities of self expression of whatever it is that the directing intelligence wants to give. Would suggest that this be written down, that this be very clear and distinct. When this one's thoughts run to doubts or fears as to whether or not this one can really accomplish*

this, this one (needs) to discipline the thinking and attention, bringing them back to what this one desires ideally. Would suggest that once this ideal has been formulated and put down on paper that then this be extended to include the physical plan of action for we do see that before there could be plans of action formed and incorporated that would be workable, there does need to be a model or seed idea around which this company is formed." *(9-14-91-7-LJF)*

The Power is in the Mental Attitude

In a small company, the business owner's thoughts and attitudes comprise the entire mental attitude of the business. But in a large company, with many employees, there is a collective mental attitude that results from the attitudes of all employees within its structure. Any group functions as well as the parts that make it up. The old saying, "a chain is as strong as its weakest link" illustrates the importance of each part to the whole. The "mental health" of a business is determined by the attitudes of the owner and employees, with everyone working together toward a common ideal and purpose.

The importance of each individual to the whole is brought out in the readings. Oftentimes, employees think their job is not significant, but as the following reading will show, the attitude of each individual makes up the attitude of the company and this affects the potential customers. The common attitude which was adversely affecting this company, a car dealership in a major midwestern city, was a lack of self worth. As a result, all employees were poor in their use of resources – goods, money, and time. The reading stated:

"Each individual in this company does waste time and is not efficient in their job from the president to the cleaning people."

Each individual's problem was not "his own," but was contributing to the condition of the entire business.

> *"...we see that each one of these ones as individuals is experiencing and bringing about within themselves some sense of lack of worth in correlation to themselves as well as to their work. We see that this causes a lack of cooperation with their desires.....We see that each one has failed to recognize their importance and fails to see the importance of cooperation with one another and communication with one another and thereby we see that this does influence the customers of this company also, for we see that it brings about an image to them of a lack of organization within this company as well as a lack of concern of those who are attempting to sell their product towards the ones who would be buying. We see that these ones do not show a concern towards each other when customers are present and we see for this to be very readily noticed by those who are interested in the products that these ones have. We see thereby that there is a skepticism and distrust which is built upon the part of the customers towards the sales people within the company....We see that it would be beneficial as individuals as well as a group for these ones to begin putting some attention upon the building of self-respect and the recognition of the self-worth with themselves as individuals. Then begin to build some pride and respect toward the company and the business that they are in." (3-25-83-1-CSR)*

In another reading, it was a shock to the business owner to discover that one of his favored employees was pregnant. He was wondering why her work had fallen off, when previously she had been a great asset to the company. It was a relief to her to have her secret "come out of the closet", for in hiding this from her boss it had indeed affected her work in a negative way. This illustrates how even one employee affects the whole company.

When employees understand their importance they are motivated to do good work. Many bosses struggle with the issue of motivation, trying to find incentives for their workers to perform well. Most people are strongly moved when they can imagine a personal benefit, as the following reading for a Chicago advertising firm suggests:

> *"We see that each person involved in this business has their own motivations, and we see for the most part that this is not merely financial support or security. We see that most of the individuals involved have their own reasons in terms of self-development or self-expression and this is a very strong building block that could be developed as these ones would begin to communicate more."*

The problem with personal motive is when it is too self-centered, when one person pushes another aside to fulfill his own desires or thinks of himself first. The Business Analysis for this company recommended that a strong leader could provide a connecting link for separate individuals to aspire toward common ideals:

> *"We see that there are very strong and dynamic personalities involved in this company and we see that they each have very definite ideas about what they want to produce. We see that it takes very strong leadership to cause these ones to work together as a group and all the factors that are necessary do exist within the company as it is now. It is merely a point of each one beginning to want to excel and to be better and to do so for a common good. This is the greatest thing that is lacking at the present time period [and is needed] for causing this company to grow and mature." (6-18-91-1-BGO)*

As each employee develops his or her strengths and talents, he or she will positively influence the business. In one business, a restaurant, the individual workers had ideals for the company and no matter how small their position in the company, they cared about its growth. As a result, the entire company benefitted. The analysis noted that most all people involved in the company had the goal and purpose of the company in mind, but pointed out the need for the individuals involved to establish personal goals and purposes so they could expect to attain something for themselves that was in alignment with the company's goal. This would enable each one of the employees to not only recognize that they had a personal investment within the company, but also become aware of what they as individuals could contribute to its success.

The Business Analyses are as individual as the business owners themselves. There are no blanket suggestions given to all businesses, the recommendations are geared to the specific concerns of each company. All the readings address the issue of using a business as a vehicle for learning and self-expression. In some cases, the directing intelligence purposefully uses his or her business to learn and teach; in other cases, the business has become a burden to which the owner is the slave.

The following is an excerpt from a Business Analysis for a company in Colorado whose owner is an artist. The reading suggested that her business has great potential and the more fully she uses it for her own artistic expression, the more appealing her products will be. In creating what she loves, she produces success:

> *"We see that there is a great potential in this company. We see that there is an ability to be able to provide a very positive place for expression for the directing intelligence......There is a great deal of room for artistic expression within this company. We see that for the directing intelligence to fulfill this one's own personal desires, there is a need for the use of more imagination as to how this one can use this company for this one's artistic expression. We see that sometimes this one somewhat diminishes or holds back upon how the Self personally can artistically express, and we see that there is a need for this one to realize that the more this one is using the company for artistic expression, then the more this one is going to be able to attract people to the company that would provide some of the other artistic expressions this one wants within the company...."*

The Analysis pointed out that this particular owner had several purposes for her business. Not only did it provide a vehicle for her artistic expression, it gave her a place to learn about life through communicating with different people:

> *"We see that this one needs to always have projects going that this one is personally working on in this one's own artistic endeavors. We see that the other line for fulfillment*

*in potential through this company is the learning to commu-
nicate with all different kinds of people, from all different
kinds of cultures....be able to express in many different ways
what this one has to offer and what this one's interests are,
in the value of the products that this one does offer. By
learning to communicate these different ways the value of
what this one's products offer, this one is also talking about
this one's self, for what this one believes in and what this one
knows to be true in this one's own personal beliefs are also
reflected in this one's product."*

It is interesting to note that this reading suggested the artist trust
her intuition and rely solely on her desires to choose the types of
products to manufacture. It counseled against using traditional marketing techniques and ideas.

*"Would suggest to this one that there are two different lines
of thought that the directing intelligence has in regard to the
creativity that is in this company. One is heartfelt of what
this one really wants to create, where this one gets excited
every time this one thinks about it. This one also has another
line of creative thought that is based on what this one thinks
should come out of a company like this one, what this one
thinks that the market expects from this one, what this one
thinks will sell. Would suggest to this one that this second
line of creative thought needs to be thrown out. For this
one's ideas, these are restrictive. They are not based upon
any kind of marketing research and they are basically
untrue. What would be accepted more readily, what would
be marketed more readily, are the creative ideas that this one
has that are heartfelt, that this one becomes excited about,
and that touch, not this one's artistic ego, but this one's
artistic heart. This one needs to identify these two lines of
thoughts within the self and use the ones suggested for
success. The other line of thought really is not useful in any
capacity and holds this one and this one's company back."*
(4-27-89-3-CSR)

In an analysis for a bookstore in St. Louis, the owner was

concerned that expansion of his business would detract from fulfillment of his ideals. The analysis suggested the opposite: that in order for him to be the kind of influence he wanted to be in the community he would need an expanded vehicle for his ideals. In actuality, the owner feared that if his business expanded it would lose the atmosphere he wanted to create. Suggestions recognized the owner's own search for personal growth giving ways to clearly image the unifying of his personal goals with those of his company. Both personal and professional ideals could be fulfilled by the owner learning to receive growth, and physical expansion of the business was necessary for this to occur.

Only a few years after bringing her Nashville relocation service to the point of profitability, the following owner had become bored with her business and was considering selling it. When asked about the possibilities of doing so, the reading had this to offer:

> *"This could be done. It would be somewhat difficult because of the way that this one has constructed the company. It would take more work than at the present time period it is seen that this one wants to invest. However, with some time this one could begin to create ways where it could be marketable and the easiest way for it to be so would be to bring in a kind of partner where it would be the intention of the partner to assume the business after a period of apprenticeship. This would give both this directing intelligence and the intended the partner the advantage of solidity and growth in the business itself. In other words, it would be uninterrupted as far as the clients are concerned. It would be much easier to change over all the legal accouterments that would be necessary in terms of how this directing intelligence has set up this business and it would afford this one of the directing intelligence to pass on her knowledge to someone else. We see that this one would not gain as much money from selling the business in this way for it would not be an outright sale, but because of how it's constructed an outright sale would have its limitations. The adopting of a partner and moving in that direction would be much more personally fulfilling to this one of the directing intelligence and it would in the long run also give this one a better return on the investment made." (9-27-91-4-BGO)*

An analysis for a dentist in Colorado showed that a business is only as effective as the people working within it, and the most noble ideals will manifest in a business only if all associated with it put them into practice. It stated that the owner did not have any new goals in his work. The owner was encouraged to seek new learning in his line of work. The reading suggested that by finding something of interest to him that would provide a sense of motivation, he could expand and gain something from his work and this would affect his practice. The people he employed in his office reflected this apathy. It was noted that all of the people associated with the business did not really care about their performance on the job. The owner was encouraged to evaluate his staff and replace most of them in order to have employees who would share his ideals and live up to them. The dentist promoted wellness in the individual and in order to be more effective in this area, he needed a staff that would practice this attitude. This would also serve to support his personal efforts in living up to his very high standards.

A Wyoming dentist has a similar problem – he has become stagnant in his work. Unlike the previous dentist, he does have people working for him who <u>could</u> use the business as a place to learn, who are sincere, but he is offering them little stimulation.

> *"We see that these ones have become complacent in their expansion of services, and in their desire to serve people's needs. We see that this affects the business in a detrimental manner....These ones do have a certain standard of work that they expect to be done, a certain standard of how to serve people, but it becomes mechanical...Would suggest that there be a time established monthly in which all those who participate within this company meet and discuss how they want to serve the people who come to them and also why. We see that the 'why' is most important, for that is how these ones learn...*
>
> *They have each one individually reached to accomplish goals in their careers or jobs and have accomplished them.....but have neglected to set new goals, and because of this, there has been a stopping in their own personal learning in this field....We see that there is a need for each one to*

establish purpose in their work, and this is something which can be stimulated as a group endeavor. For each one to attempt, not only for themselves but, to encourage each other to learn and to gain from their associations together and from what they do.

Unless each one is fulfilling a common dream in their own life, then they will not be personally involved. Therefore, it is important for each one of them to see how their work fits in with this dream and how they can activate those dreams in their life again." (10-3-84-1-CSR)

Many of the analyses point to the importance of the directing intelligence having a clear ideal and purpose, a dream, something to live for, a purpose for being. When the directing intelligence stimulates the employees to develop their ideal and purpose, each person in the company has a personal investment in its success. For example, the owner of a hair salon in Texas was interested in expanding operations to educate customers and help them become healthier. Her dream was to teach clients about inner beauty along with enhancing their outward appearance. Each one of the employees in this company believed in this dream, and the Business Analysis recommended formal communication to bring it to fruition:

"We see that there needs to be more communication between these ones and it would be of benefit for there to be a time set aside on a weekly basis for there to be that kind of communication. Each has their own areas of talent and expertise and when they are brought together and discussed there could be new avenues created which would be the fulfillment of their desires, both individually and collectively. In this way the company would evolve another step and have a momentum or rhythm which resonates to that of those that are producing it. This would lead to greater fulfillment individually and to greater profits in the business itself. It would also lead to a much higher quality of service where everyone would benefit more, these would produce a kind of contentment, more repetition of business, and more people being brought into this business." (12-12-91-16-BGO)

Many of the business owners ask if particular employees have a goal and purpose compatible with the company's ideal. In some cases they do; the employees love their work, want to grow within the company and want the company to grow. In other cases, it is simply a job they do for money. An advertising agency had recently undergone major changes in the number of personnel. The owner had reduced the number of employees from twenty-seven to nine and he asked if there would be an excessive negative impact if weak personnel were replaced. The reading analyzed the situation in this way:

> *"We see that there will be reactions upon each person involved in the business. We see the strongest reaction would be restimulation of fear that their job will be in jeopardy. This could very easily be circumvented by reassurance directly of the work that each individual is doing that the directing intelligence intends to retain. There needs to be this kind of communication anyway. There is the tendency for the directing intelligence to be too aloof and to expect the business to run itself. This is much of the reason why this one has the business on the mind most of the time that this one is awake. It is because this one does not express the ideas that this one has in the mind when it is appropriate on the job, therefore this one continues to hold the ideas in the mind and they cycle, looking for a means of expression."*
> *(6-18-91-1-BGO)*

This employer also asked questions about individual employees' job performance with exceptional results. The first was a general query concerning employed artists' resistance to leadership from anyone other than the owner.

> *"For the most part this has been addressed. We see that in regards to what is being termed the artist or those who work from spontaneous creativity, we see that they tend to be highly self-centered. However, with the idealism that has already been addressed and with the rounding themselves in terms of recognizing (their unique skills) there could be a greater understanding of their creative abilities and there-*

*fore greater control of them, there would not be such
hesitation or such a fight. We see that at the present time
period they are somewhat ego-centered because of insecurity in regards to whether their work will be acceptable or
not. This could be easily remedied by reassurance and by
greater communication from the directing intelligence to
these ones. In terms of the communication between these
ones and the coworkers, this has been addressed in terms of
everyone in this company needing to become more concerned
and more aware of how their individual positions relate to
the position of others. Every position within this company is
needed. Therefore the people who fill the positions are
needed to perform their function in order for the business to
be a whole, functioning unit. When any part of the business
does not fulfill its purpose, there is immediate and detrimental
effects experienced by the remaining parts. There is a need
for these ones to understand this and therefore to recognize
their own sense of self importance. (6-18-91-1-BGO)*

In asking questions concerning specific employees, suggestions were
given both to the employee and the owner for improvement of performance. The woman assigned to outside company purchases blamed
delays on coworkers rather than pressing suppliers to deliver on schedule. The reading revealed this woman does not enjoy her work and of
all employees she was working only for financial security and for no
other reason. Suggestions were given for stimulating a selfish motive
so she would have a reason to perform her duties with greater care and
success. A copywriter was described as willing to express his opinions
but unwilling to see projects through against the schedule. The reading
suggested clearer communication from the owner to the employee. The
employee's difficulty in following through on projects was not from
laziness or rebellion, rather he often did not understand or recognize the
owner's expectations for his performance. Another question concerning an employee who claimed she couldn't do a task because she's
sensitive resulted in this feedback:

*"Would suggest that this one manipulates others through
the emotions, and we see that this has been a long-standing*

pattern that has often worked for this one and therefore this one continues to do it. Would suggest that the directing intelligence could develop a sense of humor in regards to dealing with this employee. This would aid greatly in that this one would not take seriously many of the emotionally manipulative comments that the employee makes and would attempt to put them into perspective. It would be important that the directing intelligence not make fun of the other one, but there be a kind of levity and a kind of objectivity that this one would lend. There would be encouragement of this one's expectations that the employee can indeed accomplish the task at hand; that this one can indeed direct the sensitivity as it is referred to in the work and could make the work even better."

The owner of a national magazine discovered untapped talent in an employee when asking questions.

"We see that in comparison with the others involved in this group that this is the one who has some knowledge that is not being used. This is in regards to ideas concerning market- ing. We see that part of this is because financial security is very important to this one, more so than it is to the others involved, and therefore much of this one's attention is directed toward money. We see that although this one is highly creative and has very strong practical skills and reasoning skills, this one's motivations are very strongly toward money and this is more so than others in this group. Therefore, this needs to be recognized and the strengths from this used for we see where the others might have blind spots, this one is able to see and bring up issues that need to be considered." (7-11-91-1-BGO)

Occasionally, a reading will show that employees are actually being destructive to the company, as in the following excerpt:

"We see that there is much theft at the present time in this business; we see that most of this is not in money but in goods. We see that this is causing some financial loss to the

> *company, but even more importantly, this is taking away*
> *from the dignity of the employees and the dignity of the*
> *company and therefore is reflecting the loss of value to the*
> *customer." (9-1-82-1-CSR)*

This is one of the benefits of a Business Analysis: identifying areas of waste, areas to change so the business operates most effectively. Often, adjustments to make are fairly simple. In some companies, the directing intelligence has clear goals and the primary change to make is to share the goals with the employees. In other cases, the directing intelligence has vague goals and needs to clarify them. Sometimes, the directing intelligence is too easily influenced by other people and needs to be more of a leader in causing goals to manifest. One analysis cited that all those involved with the company were very stimulated by their work and saw much value in planned goals. Their collective effort to cooperate required greater leadership and direction on the part of the owner. Leadership was described not in the area of physical effectiveness, but rather in response to the need for moral support and encouragement for employees to receive a greater idea of responsibility.

The kind of leadership within a company determines its direction. Oftentimes, the directing intelligence doesn't fully understand what makes a good leader. One reading suggested that the directing intelligence went overboard in wanting his employees to have a sense of ownership in the company:

> *"We see that the directing intelligence within this company*
> *does have an art of involving as many individuals as this one*
> *desires in thinking that they run or own the place. We see*
> *that this is a very beneficial inclusion of people, but we see*
> *that there is a need for this one to maintain just a little bit*
> *more authority than what this one tends to do. We see that*
> *it is important for this one to realize that although authority*
> *can be overbearing, authority can also provide a sense of*
> *leadership, and it is not only leadership in making sure that*
> *a job is done well (for the people in this company do good*
> *work, so they do not need that kind of authority over their*
> *shoulder), but they do need the kind of authority of leader-*
> *ship of the maintaining of morale, of developing goals and*

*purposes, of communication, working together towards a
common goal, which can only be provided by leadership.
The directing intelligence needs to be a little bit more
authoritative to be able to accomplish these needs." (10-3-
84-1-CSR)*

Another analysis suggested that if the directing intelligence
were more firm in his own ideals, it would benefit not only his business
but his whole life. It suggested the owner stop being afraid of standing
up for what he believed in, to be willing to stand up for it with himself,
with his employees, with the people that he came into contact with and
with society. The owner was encouraged to start making a stand in terms
of not only practicing what he thinks is correct, but holding firmly to his
ideals by expecting those around him to do likewise.

Reaching Potential Customers

We have shown the importance of the mental attitude of the
directing intelligence and all people who are associated with a business.
The thoughts one practices affect all areas of life, including the emotions. To many people, this is a novel idea, for we have been taught that
"feelings" are unexpressable and "just happen". I have even heard the
idea that how we feel determines what we think. In fact, our thoughts
cause our emotions. Used productively, the expression of emotion will
cause an idea to burst forth into manifested glory. Have you ever been
excited about a new idea, and bubbled over with excitement to share the
idea with a friend? Or have you perhaps bought a product from a
salesman who believed in its value and showed you how much he loved
it with his enthusiasm? Just like there is a collective mental attitude
within a business, there is collective emotion, formed by the way all the
people within a company use (or misuse) the expression of emotion.

In one company, the directing intelligence (a physician) did not
want to admit that emotion played any part in the services he provided,
although he was aware that he had personal feelings toward or against
some of his staff people. Instead of denying his feelings, the analysis
suggested he use them for greater productivity.

"The directing intelligence has been somewhat afraid of personality conflicts and has not wanted to seem prejudicial or playing favorites. We see, however, there is a need for the directing intelligence to realize that personality and how personality is expressed is at least 50% of this one's business, whether this one wants to admit that or not. This one needs to hire people that this one likes–that this one likes their personality–for if this one likes the personalities then this one's customers will probably like these personalities. There is a need for this one to realize that the skill is important but also in this one's business the personality of the people that this one hires is important and it is important that, because it is a small company, people within it get along and work together. Therefore, it is suggested to this one that in hiring process and in whom this one has working for the Self, that this one really choose people that this one would enjoy working with and that would produce the kind of environment that this one favors within the office. Would suggest to this one that there is a place for these kinds of decisions, and that it is not prejudicial or demeaning in any kind of way." (5-16-89-1-CSR)

Similarly, an analysis for a beauty shop recommended admitting the value of emotional warmth to attract customers:

"We see that for the most part there is a genuine concern that those employed in this company do have for one another and for those that these ones serve. We see that this is not always shown. We see that many times there is a holding back and we see that this is from any variety of hesitations or fears upon individuals' parts.

We see that there is much more that these ones could accomplish by being more open and honest and by allowing the caring they do have to be expressed. This is important to each one of these as individuals. It is part of why they are together and we see that it would also open the doors to many other clients that would respond to this kind of open attitude. We see that emotionally there is some retardation inasmuch

*as there is a holding back of the emotions upon the parts of
the employees and we see that this is an attempt to maintain
objectivity and to appear in a way they believe will be
pleasing to their clients. We would suggest there is an
element of this which is of benefit but many times it is not
used, it is rather misused. And there are limitations that the
employees begin to create in terms of what they can and
cannot express, which causes them difficulty. Again, as
there would be more of the open caring displayed and this
displayed through the emotions as well, there would be a
greater satisfaction experienced in the employees and a
greater fulfillment in the work that they do." (12-12-91-16-
BGO)*

In a few of the readings, the difficulty was that the directing
intelligence denied his own emotions and refused to acknowledge the
expression of emotion within the business. As a result, customers were
treated with indifference, which was hurting the business. One analysis
pointed to the interaction between employees as being emotionally-
charged. Most of the time the emotions were seen as either in conflict
or they were being ignored. The suggestion was given for employees
to stop denying the emotions held in regards to each other and in regards
to their individual jobs within the company. By admitting, recognizing,
and expressing emotions change could occur which would make the
business atmosphere more pleasant for employees *and customers*, thus
increasing business objectives. The analysis went on to say that this
emotional conflict was the reason the business had lost many customers,
for people become uncomfortable doing business with them.

The value to a company of emotional expressiveness by its
employees was addressed in a reading for a health clinic in Australia. An
innovative concept, the business was formed to educate people in self
esteem and confidence while teaching ways to improve health and
weight control.

*"We see within the emotional system that there is excitement
that these ones have in what they are wanting to produce. We
do see that this excitement is very infectious and that this
does draw other people to these ones. But we see that*

*because there has not been formulated the very clear ideal
that often times these ones become distracted by their own
emotions for we see that these ones can very easily be drawn
into other ideas and projects that do have value but are not
necessarily related to the primary function of this business.
Would suggest, therefore, in these ones formulating a clear
ideal that when there is the emotional excitement these ones
determine if what they are being excited about is directly
related to their ideals and purposes or if this is a distraction
or if this is something these ones would want to add, or if this
is another ideal that these ones would want to form and
establish in a separate business."* (7-10-91-1-LJF)

As you can see, this approach to business is different from a traditional
business analysis. Many people consider emotional expression "unpro-
fessional". Here, the readings point out the validity of the use of emotion
for effectively serving customers. Again, this is not a blanket recom-
mendation, it is geared to the attitudes and expression of that particular
business.

Tell it Like it Is

In some cases, business owners are effectively providing leadership but may not value what they are doing that works. By taking
themselves for granted, they miss out on developing self worth. One
analysis told a restaurant owner that she had a difficult time receiving
the admiration of her employees. This affected what, how, and when
she would give direction to her workers. It was suggested she recognize
that what she communicated to her employees was very much listened
to and very much respected. When the restaurant owner heard this
analysis, it paved the way for her to enjoy her work to a greater extent.
She worried less and appreciated more of the interaction with her
employees and customers.

Business owners who are considering a Business Analysis
should be aware that these readings are honest and will "tell it like it is."
On occasion, a reading will uncover serious problems that need correcting. The following business was facing severe legal problems and the
directing intelligence was refusing to face the facts:

"We see that this company is experiencing a great deal of legal difficulty at the present time. We see that this has been due to the negligence and ignoring of facts upon the part of the directing intelligence. We see that throughout the time that this company has been in existence, there have not been the proper channels gone through to even really legally establish this business in the capacity that it is. We see that this one is experiencing a great deal of pressure because of this and we see for there to be the searching out of many individuals outside of this business as to the legalities and as to the validity of the business practices of this company. We see that there is a very definite need for there to be the cleaning up, so to speak, of past business. We see that there is the need to deal with those things that have been put off concerning legal matters.

Would suggest to the directing intelligence of this company that there cannot just be the ignoring of these legal notices and matters, for they are real and action will be taken upon them. Ignoring them is not going to help, for there will still be action upon them. We see that these individuals outside of this company have very definite intentions of doing this."
(2-14-81-3-CSC)

Another business had great financial problems. The owner was a "taker" who treated his employees poorly and had little concern for his customers. He viewed the business as a place to get money rather than a vehicle for providing service. As a result, the business was losing money. The owner was born in Greece and was quite superstitious. He was convinced he was under a curse which was causing his problems! In the course of his Business Analysis, he asked if a curse had been placed upon him or his business. The reading replied in the affirmative explaining that it was not a curse that was placed upon him by another person but rather something he was doing himself. It related that the "curse" was his own attitude of negativity, particularly those of punishment or thinking that he should be wronged for the wrong he had done to others. Although the answer was a shock, it did stir this man to admit the ways in which he misused people. He believed that there was a reason for the decline in his business, and the reading brought to his

attention the need for *him* to change rather than blaming some uniden-
tified external power.

The owner of an Alaskan firm producing films and promotional
items for companies world-wide felt a conflict of interests between his
desire for self-expression and creativity in producing the product and his
recognition of the need to make money to pay for his material needs.

> *"Would suggest to this one these are not in opposition, that
> this one will think they are in opposition as an excuse to
> refuse to organize this one's thinking, to refuse to direct the
> energies toward the manifestation of this one's dream. This
> is part of the fear that the reality of the business will not
> match what this one envisions. This is not so. These two
> ideas that have been proposed are not in conflict. They can
> very much be in alignment. Would suggest to this one of the
> directing intelligence that this one has the availability, this
> one has the vision, this one has the desire. It is some of the
> skills that this one lacks in being able to cause the fulfillment
> of his own desires as well as to be able to offer something to
> others which they in turn do want."*

When the owner asked how to change the financial burden of the
company, the answer was very direct, reiterating points made earlier in
the reading:

> *"As has been spoken of, this one is not the one to respond to
> the financial dealings of this company. This one needs
> someone that this one can trust. This could be in the form of
> an independent investor but it is not necessary for the
> success of this company. What is necessary for the success
> of this company is the directing intelligence's willingness to
> commit to the projects that this one envisions and commit to
> the manifestation of them. We see that this is this one's
> strong point and it is where this one's heart lies therefore it
> is what this one needs to be doing.*
>
> *In terms of having a whole, functioning company, this one
> then needs to draw together individuals who believe in the
> same product or dream that this one does and who would*

*have different talents that would help work to aid in the
manifestation of it. Or it could be the seeking of one or more
financial investors. The money really is not a problem as
long as this one intends to complete what he starts. As long
as this one is committed to manifesting the dream he holds
this will become apparent to others whom this one would
want to gain financial backing from whether this is through
a loan or personal contact through someone else or through
a group of people who want to invest in this project. Once
they are thoroughly sure that this one will follow through
upon what he wants, there will not be any difficulty in
regards to gaining financial backing, gaining willingness of
support for this project and there will not be any difficulty in
terms of making revenue." (1-23-91-20-BGO)*

People who are in business to fulfill their ideals are concerned
with making money so that they can expand the services they provide.
All the readings address the issue of profit, aiding the owner to find ways
to eliminate waste and increase income. In some cases, there are
materials wasted; in others, time is wasted because the workers are
disorganized. Sometimes the waste is in terms of untapped resources.
Often there are potential talents or markets that could be used to a greater
extent for increased productivity. The reading will pinpoint specific
areas to change to get the greatest use of resources available. For
example:

•For an art business, the analysis suggested finding an ap-
praiser, because the owner could charge more for her paintings and art
calendars. It also suggested using a different printer than the one she
employed, for she could receive higher quality printing for a lower cost.

•A restaurant owner's analysis suggested keeping abreast of
suppliers whose prices changed so rapidly she could find the best deals
by checking prices weekly.

•A specialty food store was told that they could charge more for
their unique products if they looked for different places to market them,
such as local hotels with international clientele.

•An electrician was told he could save time by visualizing an entire job in advance; he would then know to have all the supplies he needed and wouldn't waste time running out at the last minute.

•A physician found out that he was a poor judge of character and could increase his profits by being more choosy with extending credit. He had too many patients who were not paying their bills and had no intention of doing so. The analysis suggested that it was okay for him to turn patients down who would not pay for his services.

•A bookseller's analysis told him to order books in which he had a personal interest, for those would be easiest for him to sell.

•A produce market, on the other hand, was advised to take a verbal survey of their customers to find out what the customers wanted to buy, rather than the owners only selling what they personally liked.

As you can see, the suggestions for increasing profits are specifically linked to each business. This holds true for all suggestions. In regards to advertising, for example, some businesses are advised that word of mouth is the most effective form of publicity. Analyses for other businesses recommend the yellow pages, local radio and television, or business magazines. Some business owners are told not to use media, as it would be a waste of money and wouldn't reach the appropriate customers. One business, a car dealership, was advised to use billboards and the analysis suggested the best locations for effective use of those billboards.

Any business owner wants to identify problems and correct them before they become serious. The analyses address practical matters that the owner may not have considered. In one reading, the telephone lines were inadequate for overseas communication. Since they were in the process of expanding to foreign markets, this was to become a problem. The owner of a retail store located in a mall was having recurring problems with a cash register. The analysis revealed the problem was not the machine itself, but an electrical short located three stores away. A food store needed higher voltage for their cooling equipment for, in the long run, it would cost less than what they were using. Another analysis pointed out that the building foundation was inadequate; there was water seeping around it which would lead to eventual collapse of the building. The analysis very specifically described where the difficulty was so that it could be repaired. Another business had a different structural problem: the electrical wires under the floor were damaged. The covering on the wires had deteriorated so that dampness was reaching the wires causing a fire hazard. The analysis enabled the business to catch this problem that they couldn't see before it became destructive. A similar hidden problem was revealed in an analysis for a convenience store. They found out that an external awning contained a weakness that would cause it to break if there were a strong wind, smashing the glass front of the store. The business owner was relieved to discover and correct the flaw *before* experiencing a disaster.

Some of the practical considerations brought out in the analyses came as a surprise. A fast food establishment was using a chemical in their dehydrated food that was "not fit for human consumption". The analysis identified the toxin, where it was being used, and suggested eliminating it. The same business was also using a grease for frying that was too heavy and had an unpleasant taste. The analysis suggested that switching to a slightly higher priced and better quality grease would bring a great increase in customers. Another restaurant was advised to do some research into colors, for it was suggested that using certain colors had psychological effects for patrons.

An analysis can help business owners detect and change potential hazards to themselves, their employees and their customers. For example, a funeral home in Mississippi was using lead paint on its walls; in humid weather this paint released toxic fumes. A bookstore had inadequate fire insurance, and the method of storing books created traps so that people couldn't easily leave in case of fire.

One business owner, head of a publishing company, was greatly impressed and relieved at one of the suggestions offered in his analysis–to get their products copyrighted. This company produced unusual items worth over $2 million and it had never occurred to him previously that there was need for him to obtain copyrights to protect his ideas from theft.

In addition to practical suggestions, the analyses also offer personal suggestions for the business owners which will aid them, not only in business, but in any place in life. Some examples of the personal suggestions offered are:

• A restaurant owner was told to learn to relax.

• A food store owner was advised to meditate daily to build trust in herself.

• A business owner facing legal troubles was told to go forward into circumstances to learn instead of backing out, and to get psychological counseling.

• A dentist was advised to determine his purpose in life by doing his best at anything he does do.

• A bookstore owner was told he was idealistic, that there was nothing wrong with being an idealist, but he needed to add practicality to his life.

• An artist was given a philosophy of art which gave her a new way to approach her work and her view of aesthetics. It was suggested that beauty and grace in artistic expression would create a classic interest with universal appeal.

• A designer for children's apparel was encouraged to combine elements of art and education by creating clothes that would teach the child about color and texture, thus making this smaller company's product outstanding in a large market.

Your Work is a Means of Self Expression

The Business Analysis Readings provide great insight for anyone who runs a company–insight into their own attitudes, in learning how to communicate with others, in becoming more creative. A business is an entity in itself which can grow and develop and change.

The Business Analysis aids its owner to cause productive changes. It gets to the "heart" of the matter by identifying the key attitudes which interfere with growth. This insight is unique to these readings, for a traditional business consultant does not delve into the minds of people involved. These analyses also address practical concerns–finances, building structures, advertising, and so forth, empowering the business owner with a wholistic analysis of his or her company. It is no wonder that a wide variety of businesses have used these analyses to aid them in greater productivity and service. From realty companies in Louisiana to health centers in Australia, from steel companies in Arkansas to legal consultants in Kansas, from delicatessens in Alaska to Amway distributors in Illinois, any business can claim results from a Business Analysis.

In ancient societies, people were more in tune with the work they performed, for in smaller groups of people, with less industry and machinery, they had a direct connection between the effort they put forth and the end result. Today, we experience the direct cause and effect relationship between the work of our hands, hearts, and minds and the effects we produce when we craft a "handmade" item. Baking bread, weaving, embroidering cloth, sewing clothes, planting a garden, canning fruit, building a model or structure–all of these activities give us a vehicle to see the importance of our labor from the food we eat to the clothes we wear. Oftentimes, in our instant coffee, microwave, frozen food society, we forget there is a chain of events linking what we give with what we receive.

One of the benefits of a Business Analysis is reawakening our awareness that we each contribute to society and to humanity. Our "business" is the activity with which we busy our lives, the activity we perform to give ourselves to the world. Going to work every morning is not just a way to make money for physical survival, it is a means of expression, a vehicle for us to perform our appointed duty in the world. Discovering our importance to the company within which we work, to our community and to humanity, is a key to causing success spiritually, emotionally, and materially.

To be fully involved in the business we own or in which we are employed means to work with love, as Kahlil Gibran states in his philosophical work, The Prophet, "Work is love made visible."

After completing her Bachelor of Arts degree in Women Studies from the University of Michigan, Laurel Jan Clark developed her teaching and management skills leading to her current national position as Vice-President of the Board of Directors for the School of Metaphysics. Born in Denver, Colorado, and reared in New York, she has traveled and lived throughout the United States. In addition to giving her time in service to others as a Reader of the Akashic Record and Health Aura, Dr. Laurel is a well-known speaker and senior editor of Thresholds Quarterly, *the journal published for School of Metaphysics Associates and distributed to members in 27 countries.*

A psi counselor and ordained minister, Dr. Laurel holds all certificates conferred by the School of Metaphysics. Her book, Shaping Your Life, *is the best book available on the power of mind to create – the power known as visualization. In addition to contributing to this book, she is researching her husband's Health Analyses for an extensive essay to be included in the book* First Opinion, *which will be published by 1997. Dr. Laurel is also a mentor for Spiritual Initiation Sessions, weekend retreats designed to uplift and transform the consciousness of participants.*

Among the first class of students accepted for study at the College of Metaphysics fifteen years ago, Dr. Laurel is now a faculty member.

From *Business Ethics Magazine...*

"Life these days can be unsettling and sometimes just plain depressing, what with mass bankruptcies, sudden layoffs, and other recession-era woes. But we've heard of a way to inject a shot of fun back into your work: have a psychic reading done on your company–by a psychic trained to pick up capitalist vibrations. You can find one at the School of Metaphysics, a non-profit educational service organization in Windyville, Missouri. With plans one day to become four-year college, the school runs workshops on visualization and meditation that attract between thirty and fifty students each weekend, and it has been conducting business readings since its inception in 1973. ....

We'll admit it, we were curious. So we go an acquaintance of ours – Vic, the owner of a small, nine-person, advertising agency – to volunteer for a reading....A tape of the reading came back within two weeks. Transcripts followed later. The reading was relatively clear and to the point – with no moans, altered voices, or jargon. Though Vic remained a bit skeptical, he said the reading gave him some insights. 'I knew there were problems in the company but I'd never been able to pinpoint and solve them.'

The psychic [reader] began with her impressions of the emotional state of the company, saying she sensed confusion around the company – confusion she attributed to Vic's frustration at being unable to run the company as he would like. She also sensed that many people regularly brought their personal problems to work. And she picked up on a lack of communication between Vic and his employee, as well as problems meeting deadlines. 'There is difficulty in making commitments and meeting them. Work is seen as a job that has to be done by a certain time, and the creative staff resents that. They don't want to be disciplined.'

In a step unusual for a psychic, she ended with some solutions, such as advising Vic to re-focus his goals. Some of the advcie seemed a bit nebulous, as when [the reader] said employees should learn to make their emotions work for them. And sometimes the advice was impractical, as when she advised hiring a counselor to help employees 'develop more self-awareness' – a suggestion that would surely prove expensive.

We looked for insights specific to Vic's company, and we found some. For example, Vic asked about an artist who, despite good intentions, continually finishes his work late. From this bit of information, [the reader] identified defensiveness, insecurity, and excessive sensitivity in the artist. As anyone who knows him could tell you, she was right. Now how could she divine that? It seemed more than an educated guess, because being late isn't necessarily a function of defensiveness. [The reader] suggested that if Vic decided to keep this artist, he would need to give him more attention. But that might be difficult, she continued, because Vic shares many of the same negative attributes. Bingo–she was right again.

Based on our experience, if you're looking for new awareness of your company's dynamics, a business reading may be a good place to start." [Vol. 5, No. 5, Sept/Oct 1991]

"I would like to take the time to thank you for the Business Analysis that we had done by the School of Metaphysics. We have implemented many of the suggestions and it has increased our productivity in many ways. The information concerning our employees was very helpful. I do highly recommend this type of reading to other businesses." — Martha E. Fuqua, Administrator of New Woman Medical Center, Jackson, Mississippi

"Thank you for the recent business reading you did for my company.... Especially helpful to me was the specific relating of choices I could make to cause new excitement and interest for myself in the business. These had to do with expansion and seeking investment money, and were very detailed as to types of employees I could hire, advertising, taking on a partner, and available options for capitalization. This information has been critical to me in setting forth the direction I will take next in my business. I will recommend this type of reading to other business owners and plan to have another one done next year. This is an excellent evaluation to add to an annual review." — Cindi Rosenberger,
President of Executive Relocation Services, Brentwood, Tennessee

To Secure a Reading

For a quarter of a century, the readings offered through the School of Metaphysics have served to inform and enlighten over one hundred thousand people from six continents. No matter where you live, you can secure a reading at any time from the School of Metaphysics by writing to our headquarters on the campus of the College of Metaphysics in Windyville, Missouri 65783. As you have read, we have spent years refining the readings and ask your cooperation in supplying us with the information we require to serve you in the best way. When we have the correct information from you, we can guarantee the accuracy of your reading.

For any reading we need.....

•The complete name as it appears on the birth certificate for all individuals involved in the reading. *For females who have been married*, we need the first and middle name(s) as they appear on the birth certificate and the most recent husband's last name. This applies even if the female never legally accepted or used that husband's name and it also applies in cases where hyphenated last names have been adopted and are currently used.

•The name and complete address of where you will want the cassette tape of your reading sent.

•A phone number where you can be reached in case questions concerning scheduling your reading arise.

•When you have specific questions relative to the kind of reading you are receiving, feelfree to list them and the Conductor of the reading will make sure these issues are covered in your reading.

•Please remember that our readings are offered to aid you in understanding your present situations and circumstances which will enhance your soul progression. For this reason, do not ask us to make predictions on issues you have yet to decide upon. Our readings will not interfere with your right and responsibility to make choices in your life.

•In readings involving others (Crossing of Paths and Family Readings), the consent of all parties involved shows consideration for their privacy and respect for the service the Conductor and Reader are offering.

•If you have questions feel free to call us at 417-345-8411. Someone is available at this number from 8 a.m. to 8 p.m. Central Time every day.

•When you are ready to mail your request, remember to include at least the suggested minimum donation for each reading mailed. One hundred percent of the donations received for this service contribute to the School of Metaphysics educational services [see About the School of Metaphysics]. Readers and Conductors freely give their time to provide this service to others unencumbered by expectations of personal financial gain.

For Health Readings....
•Since Health Readings are scheduled on a first-come, first-served basis for Tuesday evenings, we must have the complete and exact street address of where you will be between 7 and 11 p.m. (CT) on two consecutive Tuesdays. The street address will either be a *number and street name* or a *route and box number,* plus the city and state. Post Office boxes are fine for mailing, but unless you plan to be in that Post Office box during the time of your reading, this will not tell the Reader where to locate you when your reading is done. Our reading schedules are full so in order to secure your reading, when you give us a place where the Reader will find you be sure you are there.

For Business Analyses....

•Business Analyses are given in response to requests from the owner or responsible governing board of the company. Please feel free to call us should you desire consultation on the type and phrasing of questions to ask during your reading. If you want to be present, arrangements can be made by contacting our headquarters.   You will receive a typed transcription as well as an audio cassette of the information given.

Time of Birth Readings...

Readers are trained to isolate the exact physical moment in time when the soul entered the physical body. Knowing the exact time of this commitment affords you the advantages of knowing your subconscious mind's intentions and expectations for this lifetime of learning as it is expressed in your astrological makeup.   To obtain a Time of Birth Reading we need your full name, the date of your birth as it appears on your birth certificate, and the exact street address (as described above for Health Readings) of where you were born.

Often people desire to be present for their readings. This is possible in several ways. Readings are scheduled weekly at our national headquarters. There are designated times throughout the year when people are invited to attend special weekends at our Moon Valley Ranch. Some of these Spiritual Initiation Sessions are centered around a Past Life or Health Reading given during the weekend. For more information on these sessions call SOM headquarters at 417-345-8411.

Readings are sometimes offered at School of Metaphysics centers. If you live in a city where a center is located, direct inquiries to your local director concerning the next available schedule times. If you live in an area where we have yet to establish a center and want to know what you can do to bring a Reader and Conductor to your city, arrangements can be made by writing to our national headquarters. Often readings are given in conjunction with lecture tours or at special conventions or seminars where Readers or Conductors are featured speakers.

It is a privilege to be able to access this information and offer it as a service to you. Learning how past lives can impact your present relationships and situations, how the quality of your thoughts can be transformed to ensure health and wholeness in mind and body, and how you can use your business as a vehicle for personal growth and service to others, accelerates the exploration and development of consciousness for all of humanity. These readings affirm the availability of peace, wholeness, prosperity, and enlightenment for us all. The information gained can be accessed through years of personal study and spiritual disciplines or through consulting a professional, educated and trained to access the information you desire. It is a honor for the School of Metaphysics to offer this kind of service. We look forward to making these services available to you throughout this lifetime and for many lifetimes to come.

Part III

Wisdom
from those who guide us

(T) hat friendship may be at once fond and lasting,

there must not only be equal virtue on each part,

but virtue of the same kind;

not only the same end must be proposed,

but the same means must be approved by both.

—Samuel Johnson (1750)

excerpts from
Guardian Angels
Wisdom from Those Who Guide Us
by Dr. Barbara Condron

Spirit Guide Readings

The nineties have seen an incredible movement toward awareness and acknowledgment of the supernatural. One way this has manifested is the open discussion of angels. No longer the solitary domain of those ordained to minister, now a child or a teacher or an auto mechanic is telling his personal story about encounters with an angel. Copied from classic European art, angels grace the cover of popular magazines. Far beyond the pins and posters of pop culture, that can and will fade tomorrow, rests the rich history of the concept and reality of angels.

Angels, or their equivalent, appear in some form in the literature, myths, and culture around the world. Their images are immortalized in Assyrian Bas-reliefs and Egyptian tombs. Angels are part of the religious tradition of Jews, Muslims, and Christians. The word *angel* appears nearly 300 times in the Bible, from the cherubim with a flaming sword who guard the entrance to the Garden of Eden to the angels of the *Book of Revelation*.

It was during the Middle Ages that scholars defined angels. Thomas Aquinas said they were pure intellect, neither male or female, and able to assume any form. Metatron is said to be "equal to the breadth of the world", while it is said that millions of angels can dance on the head of a pin. Their purpose is to praise God and act as an intermediary between the Creator and humans.

Saint Augustine said, "Every visible thing in this world is under charge of an angel." And so we at the School of Metaphysics have also found this to be true.

The School of Metaphysics possesses what is probably the world's largest collection of information gained from a controlled use of the inner, subconscious mind. In fact, there are over 100,000 Past Life Readings and Health Analyses on record at our world headquarters. These types of readings are the subject of the book **Uncommon Knowledge**. There are also transcripts of several hundred communications with souls who exist beyond the physical realm. These "Guide Readings" have been recorded for the profound insights they afford; insights into the reality of Spirit Guides or what many call Guardian Angels. Sharing these insights is the reason for this book.

Over a decade before "channeling" widely entered the public eye, several people in the School of Metaphysics, working in teams of two, enabled those studying metaphysics to speak with their guardian angels or spirit guides as they were described. This is the only time any form of channeling has been used for the readings offered through the School of Metaphysics. It was proven that the presence of a conductor to guide, assist, and protect the channel was an important element in the control and purity of the communication. The conductor made sure the reader was comfortable physically and secure mentally. This enabled the reader to fully release identity consciousness, moving the sense of self aside so another entity could temporarily use the reader's breath and vocal cords for communication. No physical dramatics or financially capitalizing on the skill as you may have seen during the '80's and the days of new age avatars. These sessions were closed – only between the channeler and the individual communicating with the celestial visitor.

Records of these sessions have been kept for the purpose of study. Through our research and work with Guide Readings, we have found there is only one entity at a time who serves as a companion to the person who is incarned. Over the years, there have been a few times when the guide has chosen to incarn having found a place where the lessons the soul needs to learn can be experienced. When this occurs, there is another who takes that one's place as guide for the individual. This is always an entity of equal learning or one slightly ahead of the individual in evolutionary development.

Since entities functioning as guides are of compatible understanding as the individual receiving guidance, they can offer insight and influence productive to the individual's learning during physical life. They also reflect their own stage of evolution offering communication according to their own understanding. Communication with your guide can enrich your life, and for this reason students learn how to access their own subconscious mind which enables direct communication to occur without the need for any external assistance.

Each Guide Reading reflects the individual's own developing abilities and progress on the evolutionary ladder of the soul. They also offer a clear perspective of physical life that is refreshing for anyone seeking deeper understanding. Many times these insights are universal in quality. For this reason we share these truths with the expectation that their timeless wisdom will enrich your own life. And perhaps they will prepare a way for communion with your own guardian angel.

Immediately, personally relevant to the querent, the words possess an ethereal quality revealing truth that is universally applicable. By sharing these excerpts we hope your mind will be opened and your heart warmed. We trust you will realize you are never alone. Always, someone is watching over you, someone you can turn to, someone who cares for you and your growth.

Be still. Listen. I am there.

Spiritual Amnesia

In the meantime, I became more educated about the nature and existence of spirit guides. I knew from my own experience and observation that direct and open communication with a guide occurs during the early years of physical life. This tends to fade with the onset of adolescence, until finally the adult ignores or discounts the ethereal presence. I knew this pattern was typical, but I did not understand why. I learned that losing contact with someone not incarned in a physical body is a result of placing more and more attention upon the five physical senses and the conscious, waking part of mind while less and less attention is given to the sixth sense and the experiences in the subconscious mind.

When the subconscious mind or soul of an individual chooses to accept a new physical body for a lifetime of learning, he or she begins fresh and anew. Information is received through the five physical senses continually, and the new conscious mind acts as a magnet drawing in pieces of information that will eventually be used for reasoning. From the time of birth to the time of puberty, the brain is constantly being fed information and the conscious mind is becoming coordinated to use this information in life experiences.

Throughout this physically formative time, the subconscious mind remains alert and active. Beyond controlling all "automatic" functions of the body, such as the heartbeat and breathing, the subconscious mind is a reservoir of understood experiences housed in the soul of the individual and a source of intuitive experience. Because conscious limitations have yet to be formed, these early years are a time of great psychic activity. This activity manifests in many ways, from child prodigies to "out of the mouth of babes" wisdom, from past life remembrances to predictions of future events, from absorbing the thoughts and emotions of others to mind reading.

When a child is taught to cultivate a use of the subconscious mind during the time the conscious mind is building, an inner balance and use of both parts of mind results. In this way, the child learns to use his sixth sense, often referred to as intuition, rather than becoming engrossed in the five senses of the physical thus neglecting inner communication. Such a child is taught Self respect, discrimination, honesty, and inner harmony. By reporting his inner level experiences to an educated adult, including his day and night dreams, he can learn to keep the doorways open between the conscious and subconscious part of his existence.

The inner urge for any entity is *"to be like"* for this is how we were created. This idea appears in all of the world's Holy scriptures. In the Bible, the creation of man is described as being *in the image and likeness* of his Spiritual parent, God. Thus the thinker has a divine birthright giving him the ability to create with thought which enables him to mature, to become compatible with his Spiritual parent, *to be like*. For this reason, the young, conscious mind reaches to identify with adult, authority figures in his life. Most adults give little time and energy to Self development and Spiritual fulfillment, and a child unwittingly imitates what he sees. By the time the child becomes an adolescent, he has moved away from his own early awareness of his inner existence by becoming more interested in matters of the physical and satisfaction of the senses. This produces an attachment to the physical, breeding conscious limitations which lead to engrossment in experiences. In this way, the doorways to the inner mind close until conscious action is taken to initiate inner communication once again.

For this reason, many adults do not remember early subconscious experiences. Since these are beyond their realm of current experience, they find themselves unable to relate to or understand the perceptions of a child or of an adult who has put forth effort to establish an inner harmony. With pride, many become amused by a child's description of his best friend whom the adult cannot physically sense, dismissing this as an overactive imagination. The child is faced with a choice: either trust in the perceptions of Self and seek greater insight into the nature of these experiences, or trust others by identifying life experiences in the fashion being communicated to him by adults and peers in his environment. For Human Man, most choose the latter because it seems easier to conform than to assert individuality and risk being different.

It is this sacrifice of Self awareness that causes one of the most dreaded and prevalent dis-eases in Human Man's existence — loneliness. Yet, for anyone who remembers that early childhood friend and for anyone who has attempted to keep the doorways open through inner listening, there is the constant awareness that no one is ever truly alone. Accepting and experiencing the reality of your own spirit guide is a step to curing this dis-ease in Self.

Telepathic Rapport

Through the many Guide Readings made available to students through the years, a much wiser and more expanded view of humanity and evolution has become known. Although guides are no more all-knowing than someone you may encounter in your daily, physical life, they do offer an intriguing perspective of Self's purpose for existence. Because guides exist beyond physical vibration in the inner levels of existence, their vantage point can be one of clear-sighted objectivity. For this reason, their insight is reminiscent of information gained in a Past Life Reading or a Health Analysis. Although your guide is comparable to you in terms of Soul evolution, he (or she) can often perceive life more accurately than you do since he does not experience limitations of a conscious mind. For this reason, establishing communication with your guide brings insight, joy, and contentment during your time in the physical plane. Communing can also accelerate your Soul progression, not so much for the content of communication received, although it can be most enlightening, but rather for the mental and spiritual attitude required to cause yourself to be both aggressive and receptive in inner level communication.

The means of communicating with a guide are as unique as individuals are. One student's first question to her guide concerned the way her guide might be trying to capture her attention. She asked if a ringing in her ear was a signal from her guide. The reply returned:

> *Often, I have brushed the side of your ear. I have not caused ringing.*

In response to the student's desire to establish a mutual communication, her guide replied:

> *Oh, it is not difficult. All you need to do is speak to me such as is now enjoyed. (7-5-81: neh)*

Your guide will present truth as he perceives it. He will be honest with you no matter how much you might want something to be different. As with this student, her guide did not mislead her by agreeing with her misconception that the ringing in her ear was a signal for communication. By telling her the truth, a door opened for her to seek the true cause for what could be a physical disorder. This guide encouraged the querent to speak her thoughts aloud, to communicate in a fashion familiar to her.

The most direct communication with your guide is the same utilized by great speakers. Great speakers have the ability to cause their words to describe their thoughts. By aligning their inner and outer minds, their ideas are given life beyond what is normally accepted and practiced. Such a speaker reaches his audience not only through the words he speaks but more importantly through mind to mind communication. The latter is known as telepathy. Telepathy can also occur between a parent and child who are physically separated, between a husband and wife who complete each other's sentences, between a person and a deceased loved one, and between you and your spirit guide. Telepathy occurs at any time for it is the projection and reception of thoughts from one intelligent being to another. Another guide expressed this thought in this way:

> *We communicate continuously, you know. But for special communication, mentally reach out for me. I will respond immediately. We will communicate in that fashion. It will become more and more noticeable to yourself as you, in your moments of determination and in making decisions, reach out for affirmation for encouragement. I will be immediately there. I may not always be encouraging you, if I feel it is not merited though. Honesty is the best way, you know, and you relate to it so well. (9-30-77: oaf)*

As command of telepathy improves, it becomes easier to separate your thoughts from those of others around you. Proficiency in telepathy also brings the ability to discriminate between communication from your own guide and from a disincarned "charlatan" who might be trying to attract your attention. Since we become accustomed to using our bodies and five senses in physical experience, developing communication with a disincarned entity, one who resides in the soul and does not have a physical means of expression, presents a challenge. Even with this awareness, we still want to be able to physically communicate with our guide. We use our bodies to speak our thoughts, so we desire to physically hear what our guides have to say, believing this will confirm in our minds their existence. When asked how verbal communication could be established and verified, another guide replied in the following way:

> *First of all, as in all cases, we are imminent, close to you, continuously. Sometimes my own vibration will seem very receptive to you – what you might call feminine in nature – when you need that quality, when you need that type of comfort. Other times aggressiveness is the way in which I will express myself, when you need that type of expression which is often by the way. You may think of me, select my vibration, which will please you most, because I know how*

you can accept others' suggestions and still maintain that
your own are best. So your own selection of my name will
be best for you. You will think that vibration and then will
speak out loud if you need to. I will be immediately in front
of you, for you need a place to expect me. That is where I
will be. It is a decision. So you may talk to me outwardly
if you like, and listen. You will have to listen for my reply.
It will not come as a seventh level (physical) sound. I
choose not to use it nor could you hear it if I used it. There
will be a time when you will hear me. (4-8-78: drc)

In addition to expanding our view of non-physical communication, this response answers a common question concerning the sexual
orientation of nonphysical entities. Once in a physical body, we are
tempted to use sexual form as an important means of expression, thus
our tendency to assign a gender to our guides is common. This gives us
a means of security for identification. Some guides identify strongly
with past associations shared with the individual they are guiding, and
in this way do express themselves in a more aggressive or a more
receptive manner in communication which we will explore later.
However, without the commitment to a physical means of expression,
any entity possesses the freedom to express both aggressively and
receptively as this man's guide reveals.

Although guides have volition, it becomes apparent in review-
ing conversations with guides through the readings that a true sense of
respect is offered in this very special relationship between a guide and
an individual incarned in the physical. This respect is experienced in a
variety of ways and most readily displayed by a willingness upon the
part of the guide to offer encouragement, love, and loyalty without
interfering with the individual's free will and capacity to determine the
course of his life. This is well illustrated in the following answer to an
inquiry concerning a manner of communication.

When you feel within yourself a warmth, when you find at
times comfort, when you are strongly influenced at times to
take a certain course, I am nudging you, shall we say. I will
at no time; however, hold you from what you feel you would

> *do, even though, it may not be the way I would wish you to go. That will always be your decision. I would wish for you to find trust for yourself, most sincerely. I would wish for you to see and find again the great strength that is within you and to bring forth again that part of self that was greatest beauty of yourself and that was the harmonious and beautifully aggressive projection of the male expression that I knew before and which is still very much within you. (11-20-74: mhf)*

Contrary to a popular misconception, the entity who serves as your guide is present to offer you counsel, not take control of your existence by making choices for you. One student was reminded of this when he asked for suggestions for a topic of a book he might write. His guide's response opened new vistas of awareness because no determination was made.

> *Now what are you asking me? Are you asking me to think for you? You know I will not. You think of a topic, you think of a title....When it is time for me to write a book, I will write my own. You will write your own, and it will come from within yourself. That is what the world needs, your own. (4-8-78: drc)*

Because each individual incarns into the physical to add awareness to his soul of being like his Creator, the use of will and development of will power is necessary for Spiritual maturity. For this reason, a true guide will only advise in the choices of the life.

Making your own choices builds an inner sense of security. A sense of security that produces Self trust is an asset to anyone desiring Spiritual and material abundance. For a thinker, Self trust is produced by an awareness and application of the Universal Truth "thoughts are things". When you gain the understanding that your thoughts have substance, are energized by your intelligent direction, and you know each thought creatively visualized will manifest into physical form, you develop trust in your ability to learn from each experience. Self trust is imperative in communicating with someone, like your guide, who does not have a physical body to use for communication. Open communication with a disincarned entity requires self-discipline and self-control.

> *Our minds are forever linked together. Therefore, you may speak to me with verbal message or you may think to me with very concrete form, and I respond to your thought process and your words. Do not doubt the receiving that you have of myself.*

Can you give me more suggestions for trusting myself in all regards?

> *To accept your youth, to accept those places of experiences you have not yet encountered and thereby be satisfied. Be accepting also of the place where you now reside in your life. Each step of life is truly a new residence and each one is beautiful and full. Therefore, if you will know that you have lived and taken care of and created many residences and have done it very well, you will bring into yourself that sense of confidence that will give you a more trusting evaluation of your present accumulation. (7-6-80: ljf)*

Communication with your guide becomes not an issue of trust but rather one of ability. In our everyday lives, we accept the reality of a friend without question. We learn to understand others have their own desires and duties which form their lives. When we develop relationships, we offer ourselves and our friends the opportunity for greater learning by sharing ideas and action. We do not waste time doubting that our friend exists. Relations with others become a means of constant discovery and growth. The same can be true of your relationship with your guide. One guide described this acceptance in this way:

> *Recognize the fact that the existence upon planes other than the physical is real and actual, that those of us who exist within this plane progress, serve, learn, understand in much the same fashion as yourself. Seeing it in reality rather than as a thing of partial knowing and partial doubt*

will help you recognize I truly exist. And also, that I exist through my choice, with the sole primary purpose of aiding you, loving you, and being one with you in every expression of your own existence at this time. I have the understanding that with all of my attention focused upon yourself and your experience, that which is needed by myself need not be of my concern for it will be given to me as I utilize your own progression and give to you what I have gained; therefore, we are united continuously. If you wish to specify a time of communication, the time before you meditate upon the Creator there is a short time in there which we might commune. See me however you wish in whatever bodily shape you are pleased with. I will exist within it. Believe that our communication is actual and do not imagine for one second that it is not. (10-5-75: rkl)

Acting on your beliefs produces a knowing in Self. This builds an understanding of trust. Self trust accelerates individual soul progression and assists in building inner communication that will aid you in creating a rapport with your guide. Such rapport produces a free flowing communication which is both given and received in a most satisfying fashion as evidenced in this amusing excerpt.

We communicate rather well. All you have to do is think to me. You know I do not perch upon your shoulder and dissect every thought that you have. Everyone needs some privacy. But when you think to me, when you want to communicate with me, I am immediately attentive. When you are not thinking to me I am also attentive, but in an aggressive way, projecting from myself to you. That is my function you know, and my duty and my greatest joy. (6-6-76: gbm)

People respond to the idea of having another who knows the way they think and their innermost secret thoughts in different ways. For those who feel victimized by thoughts they consider "bad" or "evil", the idea of a listener is intimidating. For others who have nothing to hide, the idea is stimulating and humbling. For the former, the presence of your guide can serve as a reminder to cause your thoughts to be of a higher caliber, of a more positive nature. For the latter, you will find great comfort in the sharing and even greater insight into how each thought affects all others around you.

During my session with my guide, I wanted to hear how she had viewed our communications. Expecting that her existence was very different from my own, I desired to learn about her, her experiences and her viewpoints. With full memory and trust in our many encounters, her reply was in part expected and in part illuminating.

> *As you, I love variety and something refreshing and new.*
> *So I must confess I am not consistent in my expression to*
> *you. It is in many forms. It is in your thoughts sometimes.*
> *It is in the pen you hold in your hand. The times it flows*
> *from your mind when you think, "Did I think that"? There*
> *are many ways I hope you do not mind my variety.*

I understood what she was saying, noting the many times of self-initiated thought and the times of thought "coming from nowhere". My fellow classmates found it amusing that my writings might not be coming from the person they knew, but rather be "channeled" copy. And I also laughed, being secure in identifying the difference between my thoughts and those of others, just one of the benefits of a daily investment in spiritual disciplines.

It was also important to me at that time, to verify the many early conversations with my guide during childhood, so I asked during the reading if we had communicated when I was young. She replied in this way:

> *You know we did. How we've pondered over those times in*
> *thinking back. It was truly an experience. I could feel as*
> *young as you were then, and I feel as you are now. The*
> *thought of time and age is interesting to me. (5-1-76: bgo)*

I found her answer to be mentally stimulating and spiritually challenging. Her words gave me a taste of life from her perspective, a perspective unemcumbered by the temptation to be engrossed in physical matter. Contemplating the everyday structure of a guide's experience expanded my thinking beyond self-imposed limitations. I began to relate to her existence as similar to my own experience during dreamstates. I found my understanding of the continuity of life enriched by a deeper recognition of the nature of consciousness and the growing realization that there are indeed other planes of existence beyond physical time and space, and other entities who inhabit those places.

Timeless Wisdom

Our need for a guide varies according to our awareness of their existence, our willingness to pursue inner harmony and communication, and our skill in using physical experiences to produce understanding of Self. When we embrace learning and pursue that inner level relationship with our guides, we find their perspective refreshing and their wisdom poignant. Whatever our need, we can converse with our guide with full expectation of honesty and truth relative to progression in our learning.

For any issue in life that will lead us to a greater understanding of our purpose for existence, we find avenues available to us when we open our hearts and our minds. Communication with a guide can be developed into a cooperative venture for guides do offer us the Truth they perceive. For instance, when one individual facing problems in understanding self value asked her guide for counsel, the reply came in the following way:

> *It is a curse of humanity to find a difficulty with this concept. Self value and the understanding of it is never the same from one moment of your life to the next. As you reach each step of first recognizing that you are a Self, then beginning to know about what that is, the definition changes. I think that I have overheard a phrase that puts it well, "When you learn the answers, they change the questions." Therefore, Self value for you now would simply be having a true sense of satisfaction in yourself for what you have done. (7-5-81: neh)*

Having applied metaphysical principles to her life, this woman was aware that attachment to ideas and situations of the past often hindered her recognition of self-value. She had actively been reaching to use the past for learning while living today and building tomorrow. With this is mind she asked her guide, "What kind of progress do you see in my attitudes of attachment?" She was surprised by the answer she received.

> *I would make a comment on what that attachment is. The attachment is the result of leaning heavily upon those whom you know to tell you that you are good, that you are appealing, that you are loved. The qualities which are in you that caused you to create those friendships and relationships are not taken away when separation happens, but are still very much within yourself; therefore, can be used to bring into the Self and your environment new and varying friends who can offer you a new reflection of your Self. Therefore, you will never be without friends or without those who love you. For if you have done it once, it can be done again. (7-5-81: neh)*

Attachment will express itself through the emotions of the individual experiencing it. When desires are perpetually denied thus remaining unfulfilled, attachment is the result and it is attachment that keeps us bound to the earth plane and cycles of reincarnation. One student had found many of her difficulties in life centered on her need to understand her emotions. She was aware that to more fully use the inner levels of consciousness, she would need to refine her ability to direct the action of her emotions. Her guide offered this instruction:

> *Examine them (the emotions). You realize that it is neces-sary to experience emotion even though at times it is not pleasant. In order to come to a real true understanding of it so that you can place it in a place, in a perspective. So that you can look at it in a very clinical fashion and as you progress in your realization of who you are, you will regard it as a very valid and purposeful tool. Through your*

*experience of it, you will gain knowledge and wisdom that
will enable you to help many others. Emotion is like
attention–you put it where you want it to go, but it takes a
lot of practice. (5-1-78: gdm)*

By developing the use of our mind and its attention in our
physical experiences, we discover constants which can lead us to
comprehension of the Universal Laws governing our existence. One of
these constants is change, for change is the very nature of the physical
plane of existence. With experience we realize change can be caused by
the use of volition, and when it is not we find situations and circumstances in our lives which demand that we change to accommodate our
need for learning.

Although your guide exists beyond space and time as we
measure them in the physical, they too are subject to motion and
acquainted with the nature of change in a way compatible to your own
learning. When asked if there is any way to make the process of change
smoother, one guide offered the following as a way to use attention more
fully.

*I can not make it smoother. I can offer you ideas, suggestions,
as to how to regard change in yourself. You very easily
slide into a place of comfort in your activities within your
life and hold on to them because this is where you have
proven yourself externally. The new points, the changes
that come toward you, reach out for your attention. They
wait for you to reach out to them, yet the ties of your
hesitation pull you back. You feel that you have proven
yourself in certain fields of endeavor and therefore this
must be clung to. Not so. You can also reach out for new
worlds to conquer within your own world.*

*You have great force and expressiveness within yourself.
You have great beauty and poetry within your mental
processes. Allow this to be expressed outward. Don't
stand in any one place. Your energy, your enthusiasm, your
love that is so full of yourself can be truly contagious and
affect many if you will offer it out to them. Try pouring as*

much attention and love and beauty upon adults as you do children. Do not question your own authority, this is where you pause, where you hesitate. You do not question your authority in working with your children, but you do question it in working with adults....respect your own experience in seeing your own maturity. Take your own authority and express it outward. Become a stability point for others who have not reached it yet. Offer yourself as that point of authority. (4-18-79: mrb)

As we reach to identify what we know, thus becoming centered in our own authority, a birth of expectation of what can be occurs. Lovingly created thoughts become our means of producing a positive, productive life that accelerates our evolution. For this to become a reality in our daily life necessitates admitting points in our thinking that are in need of change. Until this is accomplished these points remain unconscious in our thinking, escaping our conscious discernment. To release negativity means to face those thoughts which fail to produce desired results as this man's guide instructed.

Remember that negative is a word that describes something. Before you can recognize what is negative, you have to recognize the thing itself. Therefore draw out of that unconscious, as you call it, part of your mind, the things that you have placed there. Look at them, there is this thing and that thing and another thing. These are things to observe; 'Why then do I feel negative about these things.' You cannot release a quality of emotion until you find the thing you are reacting to. Is that not true?

That is true. So if I come to a better understanding of these qualities, they will depart as I wish?

Even before you can understand you have to know what it is you are trying to understand. You have to take the things out of the unconscious. I have placed this in. It is a fact. I will pick out this fact and look at it. I am reacting to this fact in this fashion and, therefore, I do not understand it.

*You have placed in the unconscious mind time periods of
activity. This activity you are reacting to still in a negative
fashion. Review the activity itself, observe why the activity
was what it was. Remember, at the point of that activity you
had a certain state of development. That's all. So your
decisions which were made at that point came from that
state of development, and that is all. Why react negatively
to a fact. Look at the fact and release it. Recognize your
place of development during those periods and say, here is
where I am, that is where I was. Was no longer exists for
you, only now. How can you be negative about a thing that
no longer exists? (4-8-78: drc)*

One of the best ways to replace negative patterns of thought
with more productive, positive ways of thinking is built during daily
meditation. Meditation becomes a sacred time of directing all of the
mind in concentration toward knowing the Creator and aligning the
whole self. Your guide knows of your thoughts and actions, thus your
guide can offer you suggestions based upon your efforts toward enlightenment.

*You have great ability to reach into yourself within medi-
tation many times. I feel that perhaps you are somewhat
scrupulous or overscrupulous in this direction and fail to
appreciate your ability to communicate with the Self. I feel
that you also fail to appreciate the beauty of the Self.*

Can you give me some more suggestions as to how I
can appreciate the Self more?

*Remembering how much you have worked through the life
experience. Remembering, for example, the time when you
were truly beautiful and very wise, when you truly had
much authority and many at your feet. The beauty of
yourself was known through the land and all that was
manifested was there for you to have. Eventually this
became tiresome to yourself and through much difficulty
you came away from this action and you began to reach*

within the Self for truer understanding. Your example and your purity also was of great influence to many around you and therefore much wisdom was gained into yourself by your decisions. This is but one example of much activity and taking in of things that you have experienced in your life.

In the present time you are truly, even though I might myself be biased in your favor, you are in truth a very great beauty, within and without. Do not deny yourself this understanding. Do not hold this away from others but accept it and again use the wisdom that you have earned to express it into your life and to bring joy into your students. (7-6-80: ljf)

As you will note, your true guide will readily admit the points of limitation still existing in their own learning. This is demonstrated by the admittance of bias in the selected excerpt above. Because each guide is compatible in learning and evolution to the individual they are guiding, their direct grasp of objective truth is sometimes limited. Merely because an entity does not possess a physical body to use for communication does not make that entity all knowing. However, because your guide is compatible with you, he (or she) does hold a very special place in your life for he can offer you the experience of true friendship once communication is established.

As you progress in your evolution, you offer your guide the opportunity to learn through observation of the thoughts and activities you choose to experience. With this in mind, one student wanted to know his guide's assessment of his anticipated goals for his life. The counsel offered is of value to anyone who desires progression for the soul.

First, let me suggest that you view these goals very carefully and establish them firmly in your mind. I recognize that you have been at this. View them from an objective point of view as much as possible and then step by step begin in seeing yourself, begin to know that these can be and will be, <u>will be</u>, accomplished. See the benefit of the achievement of these goals, not only for Self but for others. See how the

> *whole benefits from the accomplishment of one. See that each entity has a place, has a vibration that is necessary to each other entity. And see how necessary yours is to others. Begin to see and appreciate the male and female expression as a working together in harmony to produce a certain vibration within this time period, for balance and harmony is what is needed. As each one becomes understanding of these expressions, this then is projected out to many and gradually harmony is restored wherever this is understood. You have the ability to project this outward; you must discover it again for yourself. I will be with you constantly and you will recognize my presence. I promise. (11-20-79: mhf)*

When you find yourself tempted to believe that you are alone in your thinking or that no one really understands you, remember there is someone present at all times whereever you are. This someone has made a commitment to aid you in your progression whether you are aware of his presence or not. Reach for communication with the one who accompanies you upon your journey toward enlightenment. Strive to make those choices in your life that will bring greater awareness of the depths of your Self and bring to your Self the skills of inner level communication. You will be richly rewarded in all ways by choosing spiritual advancement. Timeless wisdom will become yours to share.

Upon earning a Bachelors of Journalism degree from the University of Missouri at Columbia, Barbara Condron pursued her urge for spiritual knowledge through applied studies in metaphysics with the School of Metaphysics. Since earning all degrees conferred by that nonprofit educational institute, Dr. Barbara has continued her association with the School in a wide range of positions and responsibilities as a way to serve the growing needs of humanity. She is currently the CEO of SOM Publishing, Editor-in-Chief of Thresholds Quarterly, *international coordinator for the annual National Dream Hotline® project, supervisor of SOMA, and chairman of SOM Board of Directors. Dr. Barbara's varied activities recently resulted in her nomination to* Who's Who in America. *She has written many books including* Kundalini Rising, The Dreamer's Dictionary, *and* First Opinion.

Dr. Barbara initiated the Universal Hour of Peace in 1995, inviting the world including heads of state, ambassadors and U.N. representatives, corporate managers, religious leaders, university faculty, to commit themselves to peace for one hour so that we might create an hour of gobal peace. Whether teaching, lecturing, giving readings, or writing about the development of man's potential as a creator, she has stimulated thousands to open their minds and hearts to greater Self awareness.

Additional titles available from SOM Publishing include:

The Work of the Soul

Dr. Barbara Condron   ISBN 0944386-17-2 $13.00

First Opinion

Dr. Barbara Condron   ISBN 0944386-18-0 $13.00

The Dreamer's Dictionary

Dr. Barbara Condron   ISBN 0944386-16-4 $15.00

The Universal Language of Mind: The Book of Matthew Interpreted

Dr. Daniel R. Condron   ISBN 0944386-15-6 $13.00

Permanent Healing

Dr. Daniel R. Condron   ISBN 0944386-12-1 $9.95

Dreams of the Soul - The Yogi Sutras of Patanjali

Dr. Daniel R. Condron   ISBN 0944386-11-3 $9.95

Kundalini Rising - Mastering Your Creative Energies

Dr. Barbara Condron   ISBN 0944386-13-X $9.95

Shaping Your Life - The Power of Creative Imagery
Laurel Fuller Clark ISBN 0944386-14-8 $9.95

Going in Circles
Our Search for a Satisfying Relationship
Dr. Barbara Condron ISBN 0944386-00-8 $4.95

What Will I Do Tomorrow? Probing Depression
Dr. Barbara Condron ISBN 0944386-02-4 $4.95

Meditation: Answer to Your Prayers
Dr. Jerry L. Rothermel ISBN 0944386-01-6 $4.95

HuMan, a novel
Dr. Jerry L. Rothermel ISBN 0944386-05-9 $5.95

Discovering the Kingdom of Heaven
Dr. Gayle B. Matthes ISBN 0944386-07-5 $5.95

Autobiography of a Skeptic
Frank Farmer ISBN 0944386-06-7 $7.95

To order write:

School of Metaphysics National Headquarters

HCR 1, Box 15

Windyville, Missouri 65783 USA

Enclose a check or money order in U.S. funds payable to SOM with any order.
Please include $2.00 for postage/handling of books, $5 for international orders.
A complete catalogue of all book titles, audio lectures and courses, and videos is
available upon request.
Visit us on the Internet at www.som.org

About the School of Metaphysics

We invite you to become a special part of our efforts to aid in enhancing and quickening the process of spiritual growth and mental evolution of the people of the world. The School of Metaphysics, a not-for-profit educational and service organization, has been in existence for more than two decades. During that time, we have taught tens of thousands directly through our course of study in applied metaphysics. We have elevated the awareness of millions through the many services we offer. If you would like to pursue the study of mind and the transformation of Self to a higher level of being and consciousness, you are invited to write to us at the School of Metaphysics National Headquarters in Windyville, Missouri 65783.

The heart of the School of Metaphysics is a three-tiered program of study. Lessons introduce you to the Universal Laws and truths which guide spiritual and physical evolution. Consciousness is explored and developed through mental and spiritual disciplines which enhance your physical life and enrich your soul progression. We teach concentration, visualization (focused imagery), meditation, and control of life force and creative energies. As a student, you will develop an understanding of the purpose of life and your purpose for this lifetime. Study centers are located throughout the Midwestern United States.

Experts in the language of mind, we teach how to remember and understand the inner communication received through dreams. We are the sponsors of the National Dream Hotline®, an annual educational service offered the last weekend in April. Study centers are located throughout the Midwestern United States. If there is not a center near you, you can receive the first series of lessons through correspondence with a teacher at our headquarters.

For those desiring spiritual renewal, weekends at our Moon Valley Ranch offer calmness and clarity. Each Spiritual Initiation Session's mentor gives thematic instruction and guidance which enriches the Spirit and changes lives. One weekend may center on transcendent meditation another on understanding dreams, one *may center on wholistic health while another investigates relevant past lives. Please feel free to contact us about upcoming sessions.*

The Universal Hour of Peace *was initiated by the School of Metaphysics at noon Universal Time (GMT) on October 24, 1995 in conjunction with the 50th anniversary of the United Nations. We believe that peace on earth is an idea whose time has come. To realize this dream, we invite you to join with others throughout the world by dedicating your thoughts and actions to peace for one hour beginning at noon [UT] on the first of January each year.*

There is the opportunity to aid *in the growth and fulfillment of our work. Donations are accepted and are a valuable way for you to aid humanity by supporting the expansion of the School of Metaphysics' efforts. As a not-for-profit publishing house, SOM Publishing is dedicated to the continuing publication of research findings that promote peace, understanding and good will for all of Mankind. It is dependent upon the kindness and generosity of sponsors to do so. Authors donate their work and receive no royalties. We have many excellent manuscripts waiting for a benefactor.*

One hundred percent of all donations *made to the School of Metaphysics are used to expand our services. Donations are being received for Project Octagon, the first educational building on the College of Metaphysics campus. The land for the proposed campus is located in the beautiful Ozark Mountains of Missouri, less than four hours from St. Louis and Kansas City, and one hour north of Springfield. The four-story octagon design will enable us to increase headquarters staff and enrollment in our College workstudy program. This proposed multipurpose structure will include an auditorium, classrooms, library and study areas, a cafeteria, and potential living quarters for up to 100 people. Gifts may be named for the donor or be designated as an ongoing memorial fund to a family member or special friend. Donations to the School of Metaphysics are tax-exempt under 501(c)(3) of the Internal Revenue Code. We appreciate any contribution you are free to make. With the help of people like you, our dream of a place where anyone desiring Self awareness can receive wholistic education will become a reality.*

We send you our Circle of Love.